Labor of Love
One Chicago Teacher's Experience

Deborah Lynch Walsh

Writers Club Press
San Jose · New York · Lincoln · Shanghai

Labor of Love
One Chicago Teacher's Experience

All Rights Reserved © 2000 by Deborah Lynch Walsh

No part of this book may be reproduced or transmitted in any form or by any means, graphic, electronic, or mechanical, including photocopying, recording, taping, or by any information storage or retrieval system, without the permission in writing from the publisher.

Published by Writers Club Press
an imprint of iUniverse.com, Inc.

For information address:
iUniverse.com, Inc.
620 North 48th Street
Suite 201
Lincoln, NE 68504-3467
www.iuniverse.com

ISBN: 0-595-09720-0

Printed in the United States of America

This book is dedicated to the memories of Albert Shanker, John Kotsakis, and Jacqueline B. Vaughan, who taught me, and to my family, friends, colleagues and students, who continue to teach me.

Contents

Chapter I. The Early Years, 1974-79: The Journey Begins 1
    a. decision to become a teacher
    b. preparing: university & student teaching experience
    c. teaching in the Chicago Public Schools
        1. Barnard School: initiation into the profession
        2. Whistler School: learning the ropes
        3. Evers School: decision to leave
    d. becoming a professional development specialist: lessons
    e. decision on a doctorate: taking the plunge

Chapter II. The Chicago Teachers Union (CTU) Years,
1980-83: Lessons From John Kotsakis 21
    a. interview with John Kotsakis: connecting with the CTU
    b. getting published: "Classroom Stress & Teacher Burnout"
    c. creating the CTU's first professional development initiative

Chapter III. The Ph.D. Years, 1980-83: Power and
Powerlessness in Teaching 41
    a. the McPherson experience: brush with intellectual passion
    b. dissertation findings: Power & Powerlessness in Teaching
    c. going national: joining the American Federation of Teachers (AFT) staff

Chapter IV. The American Federation of Teachers(AFT)Years,
1983-91:Lessons From Albert Shanker 55
    a. the ideas and influence of Albert Shanker
    b. Developing AFT's Critical Thinking Project: promoting intellectual passion
    c. union debate: bread & butter or professional issues
    d. AFTSU: work in the AFT staff union
    e. work with AFT locals and state federations on educational issues

      f. national issues affecting schools & unions (e.g., charters, privatization, vouchers)
      g. collaborating with John Kotsakis to write a MacArthur Grant

Chapter V. Sojourn to Poland, 1991: Lessons From Teacher Solidarity 77
      a. inspiration to go to Poland
      b. the AFT's work with Teacher Solidarity
      c. bus journey around the country of Poland
      d. visit with Anna Karp, teacher educator, and friends
      e. lessons learned on this journey

Chapter VI. The Chicago Teachers Union Years, Continued, 1992-95: Quest for Union Leadership 97
      a. Chicago's 1988 Reform legislation
      b. receiving/announcing the MacArthur grant
      c. Starting the Quest Center: a new venture for the union
      d. accomplishments of the Quest Center
      e. internal CTU politics: bread & butter vs. professional issues
      f. the untimely deaths of Jacqueline Vaughn & John Kotsakis
      g. creating a union-led graduate school for teacher leadership
      h. decision to leave: going with the idea of returning to the classroom

Chapter VII. The Marquette Years, 1995-Present: Quest for Teacher Leadership 119
      a. re-entry into the school & classroom after 15 years
      b. personal teaching issues & concerns
      c. school-wide issues & concerns (LSC, PPAC, student achievement, teacher attitudes/culture)
      d. Chicago's 1995 Reform legislation
      e. reflections on reform: national vs. local issues
      f. being the schools' union representative
      g. reciprocal teaching: trying to bring research to practice
      h. selling & adopting Johns Hopkins University's "Success for All" program

Chapter VIII. The PACT (ProActive Chicago Teachers) Years, 1995-1996: Starting a Movement 143
      a. decision to run for union office
      b. reaching out to the membership

  c. PACT campaign issues
  d. the incumbents' response
  e. the results and next steps

Chapter IX. An Open Letter to CEO Paul Vallas from a Chicago Teacher, 1997 163
  a. The Teaching "Profession"
  b. the potential to be change agents
  c. the Chicago reality
  d. the Saturn model
  e. accountability with responsibility
  f. the role of the teachers' union
  g. the challenge

Chapter X. The PACT Years, Continued, 1998-Present: Taking a Stand 177
  a. the '96 challenge & its findings
  b. keeping interest and hope alive
  c. PACT campaign issues '98
  d. the incumbents' response
  e. the erosion of union democracy
  f. results '98 & next steps

Introduction

Life's journeys. Long stretches of open highway, dead ends, detours, forks in the road. Fits and starts, rough spots and smooth. Choices to make, always choices to make. Sometimes we can see clearly what is ahead of us. Sometimes we forge ahead blindly. Sometimes the lessons learned are obvious, sometimes realized only years later, if at all. We never know what is ahead. Yet we keep moving, keep choosing—sometimes with awe and amazement, sometimes with sadness and regret, and often without quite noticing the wonders around us.

Every so often it's good to stop, look back, look around. It's good to see how far you've come, what you've learned, before forging ahead again, hopefully, carefully, adventurously. I'm pausing here, now. The journey I am looking back on is my teaching journey, the professional path that I chose over a quarter of a century ago. It's not possible that it went so quickly. I don't feel old enough to have logged in twenty-five years in my profession. Yet I have, and I am.

What have I learned over that expanse of time? About teachers and teaching, about learners and learning, about the person that started on that road then, and who I am at this, a pause, a rest stop? What has happened to that eager, twenty-something young teacher? Like so many fresh, new teachers, college degree and teaching certificates in hand, she entered the schoolhouse door with hopes and dreams and expectations of changing the world. Were those hopes, dreams, and expectations realized and achieved, or were they dashed and disappointed? Did that young teacher and her profession grow and mature as the years flew by and the world changed so dramatically? Or not? These are the questions of this book. I know some of the answers to these questions, of course, but not all of them. Carl Sandburg said that "the past is a bucket of ashes." I'm not sure that I agree entirely with the great Illinois poet, but he had a point. It's not so easy to read the past as some think.

I am the teacher about whom I write. I write for many reasons, personal, philosophical, and political. I write to explain who I am, what I've learned on this journey, what I stand for, what I care deeply about. I write to advocate for my profession by exploring and exposing the rhetoric and the reality of urban public school teaching. I write to share one teacher's experiences, observations and reflections, for what they're worth. I also write for political reasons, to incite, activate and agitate the individuals, the groups, the unions and the organizations who are responsible for the integrity, the strength, the very future, of this noble profession.

This teaching journey began in 1974, on the south side of Chicago, in the company of a group of mentally retarded children. **Chapter One-The Early Years, 1974-1979: The Journey Begins**, details my experience in a large, anonymous public school system, the Chicago Public Schools. That induction shaped my entire professional experience. This story describes how the teachers in my first schools dealt with the trials and tribulations of schooling. What did they care about? How did they pass on the norms, the promise, the possibilities, of the profession to the neophytes? How were they treated by the administration? And what made me leave teaching, then?

From teacher to ex-teacher, **Chapter Two-The Chicago Teachers Union Years, 1980-1983: Lessons from John Kotsakis**, describes the lessons I learned about my profession from what some would consider an unlikely source, the teachers' union. In an interview with a leader of the Chicago Teachers Union (CTU), I saw the school system from a completely different perspective, the perspective of "the union." This chapter details how a belief about teacher professionalism, teacher power, took root.

From the union to the university, the journey continued, as I transformed personal experience and observation into a full length study about teacher power and powerlessness. **Chapter Three-The University of Illinois at Chicago Years, 1980-1983: Power and Powerlessness in Teaching,** raises questions, too. Is teaching a profession, or isn't it? What makes some teachers feel like they are making the difference in people's lives that they had dreamed of making? And what is it that has *prevented* so many of them from realizing their teaching dreams? Why is the dream so elusive? Why, when issues of poverty and family breakdown are so severe, and school reform so necessary, do the professionals seem locked out of the decisions about what is best for teaching and learning? Why does the term teaching professional seem like such a contradiction?

The road I took then led from Chicago to Washington, D.C., from the local level to the national level, from the Chicago Teachers Union to its national affiliate, the American Federation of Teachers (AFT). Here, another contradiction emerged, as compelling to me as the first. **Chapter 4-The AFT (American Federation of Teachers) Years, 1983-1991: Lessons from Albert Shanker**, addresses still more questions. Does the teachers' union represent workers, or professionals? Should it focus strictly on bread and butter issues or are professional issues also its concern, even its obligation? Does the union have an obligation to try to reform and renew the schools (and perhaps, the profession), or is that strictly management and government's job? The vision and the leadership of the late AFT Albert Shanker, and several other progressive AFT leaders around the country, taught me so much. What I learned from them informs much of this chapter.

My path next took me to Poland where democracy and freedom were breaking out all over. Teachers there, newly free, had great hopes for teaching and learning in a new, promising era. **Chapter Five-Sojourn to Poland, 1991: Lessons from Teacher Solidarity,** describes the inspiration and insights I gained from brave Polish teachers who had kept a movement alive, a movement to bring democracy to their country, and dignity, finally, to their profession. The comparisons and contrasts of our two countries and our experiences left deep, and lasting, impressions.

After eight years away, it was time to go home, sweet home, Chicago. I returned a different person, shaped by exciting and wonderful national and international experiences and opportunities. **Chapter Six-The Chicago Teachers Union Years, 1992-1995: Quest for Union Leadership,** details my return to the union where my search for teacher professionalism started, to lead in the creation of a center for teacher professionalism within it. It also details the internal tensions in the local union to reconcile leadership on bread and butter issues and leadership on the professional and school reform issues.

The search for teacher leadership is explored in **Chapter Seven-The Marquette Years, 1995-present: Quest for Teacher Leadership,** as I returned to the classroom after a fifteen-year hiatus working on a doctorate and doing union work. What would a return to the classroom be like after all those years? How would the national and local conversations, the summits and meetings, the task forces, the reports on school reform, have affected the real world of the school? What impact did all this have on the profession, if anything? This chapter also chronicles the efforts of the teachers at my school to do something important and proactive about the kind of education we provided to our students. So many of our students were poor and at risk of school failure. This exploration includes the trials and tribulations of these grassroots reformers as they kept faith with their commitment to meaningful, long term school reform despite the odds and the obstacles.

Chapter Eight will be discussed in conjunction with Chapter Ten. **Chapter Nine: An Open Letter to Paul Vallas from a Chicago Teacher,** is a letter I wrote to the head of the Chicago Public Schools describing the issues and concerns of the rank-and-file teachers. In it I describe the consequences of the continuing lack of professional respect, recognition or involvement of teachers in school reform issues. It explains how much management needed teachers if the system was ever going to turn around to the extent truly necessary. This letter proposed several alternatives to school reform. It advocated viewing the profession as the solution, not the problem, to school improvement.

Chapter Eight-The PACT Years, 1995-1996: Building a Movement and **Chapter Ten-The PACT Years, 1996-present: Growing a Movement,** recount the energy and the excitement of the two campaigns I have undertaken—with the incredible support of so many—to assume the leadership of the local teacher' union, the CTU. These challenges were undertaken because of the new union leadership's inaction and inability to articulate member needs, to garner for the members the professional dignity, respect and voice we deserve. This chapter explains the decline in power of the once-powerful CTU, the erosion of its members' rights, and the lack of union democracy in response to these internal challenges.

I have come full circle on my professional journey, from my classroom, to my union, and back again. The ultimate lesson for me on this journey is that the only worthy and dignified hope of teachers' power and professionalism lies in their union. The union is the *only* source of independent power that teachers have. It must work for them and for the realization of their dreams as professionals. We are *teacher union* members, professionals who are members of a union.

The issues and themes of this book—teacher power and powerlessness, teacher leadership and decision making, union leadership, educational accountability—are all issues that the union can do something about. We have professional demands and bread and butter demands. We care about our profession, our workplaces, and, most of all, about the children we serve. We want to give them the best possible service, in the best possible schools under the best possible conditions. Good working conditions yield good learning conditions. That is why teachers care so much about issues of teacher empowerment, because they empower us to realize our full potential as teaching professionals

And if our union isn't doing something about these issues, then we have to do something about the union. The jury is still out on what Chicago teachers and para-professionals, and teachers and para-professionals across the country, will ultimately choose, which direction they will want their unions to take.

And so my teaching journey is really a learning journey. What will happen to the teaching profession in the years to come? What will happen to our public schools, particularly our urban public schools filled with students who have such great needs? Will the profession and the public school system survive the efforts to privatize and voucherize? We teachers have more power than we realize. We can play an important role in the future of our schools, our profession and our union, but will we choose to use that power? The answers to those questions remain to emerge.

Another American poet, Robert Frost, wrote: "But I have miles to go before I sleep." Teacher union members might well heed this compelling line of verse. The journey continues, for us, alone, and together.

Chapter 1.
The Early Years, 1974-79:
The Journey Begins

I am a teacher. This is my story.

In the sweltering summer of 1965, I was an energetic thirteen-year-old with nothing to do. My mother wisely suggested that I ride my bike to a new school for handicapped children in our neighborhood to see if they needed volunteers. That experience at Park Lawn School in Oak Lawn, Illinois, changed my life. I loved every minute of my "work" helping severely handicapped boys and girls. One of my goals that summer was to get Timmy, a hauntingly beautiful autistic child, to smile at me. While I didn't succeed at that, I found my niche for life, and I decided then to be a teacher. Despite the continuing challenges of practicing and promoting teaching—helping it become a true profession, for me and for others—I have never regretted that decision.

My undergraduate training to become a teacher was typical of what one could find those days in a large, public university: classes with hundreds of students, impersonal professors, and lots of student anonymity. Many people claim to have avoided the teaching profession entirely because of the dire prospects of taking teacher education courses. I can relate to those stories. Many courses I took were student exercises in psyching out the teacher to decide what had to be done to get an A or a B. The most egregious example was my philosophy of education course, where passing meant getting 51% or better on four multiple choice tests. Anyone with even a rudimentary sense of statistics could figure out that the chance of passing, even if she didn't attend class or buy or read the book, was very good. I aced that course.

A course that I do remember as having some meaning involved taking field trips to two of the state institutions that, at the time, cared for severely and profoundly handicapped children and adults. I returned burning with desire and impatience to go out and help them, unable to wait for school's end. I even discussed my thoughts of dropping out of college to go to work in the real world with my faculty advisor. Thankfully, he took me seriously and convinced me not to leave academics with just one question, one that has remained with me to this day. "Sure, you can quit and go right to work," he said on that day long ago. "But ask yourself this: do you want to be the one making the decisions out there or the one being told what to do?"

He had a compelling point, though he was talking about teaching as we wish it were—teaching as a profession—not the harsh reality that so many practicing professionals in this nation's schools know only too well. I stayed in college through graduation and then moved on to save the world or so I thought.

But I'm getting ahead of myself. My student teaching experience, like that of many, was abominable. Since I was getting a dual major, in elementary and special education, I was assigned to a Chicago school for two six-week sessions, one in a regular classroom and one in a special education classroom. For six weeks, I sat and watched the third grade teacher. She never let me have a chance to teach, not even one day, not even one period. While disappointing, it was nothing compared to what I encountered in the special education classroom. It was isolated from the building (surprise, surprise!) in the school's sole mobile unit. Inside was a class for trainable mentally handicapped students, ages 6-16, contrary to the existing state regulations for the number and age span of children in one classroom. The teacher was not certified in special education. She had been the school's music teacher;

she had lost her position, and this was the only position available to her if she wanted to stay at the school. She was overwhelmed and she knew it. Her idea of vocabulary development for these children was to have them watch the Password show on television. After lunch everyone took a nap, (including the teacher). I was told there were times when the bus driver had to go around back and wake them all up at 3:00 p.m.

The teacher was receptive to ideas and techniques that I brought in from my college classes, but I realized quickly that the process was backwards. My university supervisor was no help at all. I think she showed up once, and I kept quiet about that because I was reluctant to get my supervising teachers in trouble. I just knew that this was not the way it was supposed to be. I felt sad for the 16-year-old TMH kids who were forced to take naps every day.

Now back to saving the world. I became an employee of the Chicago Public Schools. At the time you had to go "downtown" to apply for a job and to get assigned. There I was, bright-eyed and enthusiastic, with a newly minted teaching certificate in hand. Imagine both my confusion and chagrin when the woman who interviewed me sent me to a school as a teacher for students with learning disabilities (LD). I protested to her that I was not trained for LD but this didn't seem to matter to her. She informed me that this LD classroom was all they had for me. I had been told that if you didn't accept the first assignment that they gave you, you could be blackballed from the system. Dutifully, I did as she told me and reported to the school's principal. He interviewed me for a few minutes and then told me I had the job.

"But," I protested to him, "I'm not certified to teach children with learning disabilities," thinking that logic was all it would take to get me out of the situation. "I'd be doing a disservice to them."

"Then you ought to pay us to let you work here," he replied sarcastically.

I didn't care if I were to be blackballed or not. I just knew that taking that position wasn't right, so I refused it. That refusal paid off. A few weeks later a position opened that was just right for me, a class for trainable mentally handicapped children. That was the first time I questioned and challenged the Chicago Public Schools ways of doing things, but it wouldn't be the last.

So, in the autumn of 1974, I began work at Barnard School in the far south side of the city. My special education classroom there was just like the one where I did my student teaching, quite isolated from everyone else, the lone classroom in the basement. I had more students than state regulations allowed and a greater age span. Yet I loved that class and it was one of my all-time favorite teaching assignments. I was lucky to have a half-time teaching aide, and Mrs. Bright taught me more about teaching in our five years together than my teacher preparation program ever did. In fact, if I hadn't had the benefit of her wise counsel and decades of experience, I might have thought I couldn't handle the challenge of 16 TMH kids. Half of them were fighting and crying within my first 30 minutes on the job! When Isaiah tore off away from our class during a fire drill and tried to climb on the parked cars, she insisted that I go after him and show him who was in charge. When the children inevitably would fight, she guided me in finding the right help for them. When the father of one child appeared to have crossed the line in home-school cooperation, she advised me on that problem, too.

The teachers at Barnard were all gracious and generous to me. So many of them took me under their wings, as it happens in schools everywhere, in an unspoken and informal initiation into the profession. Unfortunately, some of that orientation was discouraging. They chided me in a friendly way. Monday mornings, for example, I would come into school with my arms loaded with more things to do and to try in my classroom. "One of these days you'll be just like us," they would say, "and you won't be putting all that time and effort in on weekends anymore."

I didn't understand why they would try to deflate the new recruit, and only later would I realize that it wasn't meant as discouragement. They were saying that they had been worn down by the system. The bureaucracy had eroded their own initial enthusiasm and motivation for teaching. It didn't want them to deviate from bureaucratic norms. It didn't want them to question the dictates and decisions of others on high over their daily work lives. It didn't want or need the benefits of their experience and expertise in running the schools. They had learned, relatively quickly, who had the power in the system and who did not. They also knew that their only recourse to the power reality in their work lives was to complain among themselves. You could not go up against school authorities in those days and expect to keep your job.

This was a confusing culture for me to observe and to become a part of. These professional, expert classroom teachers complained in the teacher's lounge. They never complained directly to the administration. They had no authority and no control over their daily work lives. It contradicted any notion of professional authority or autonomy I had learned or in which I believed. This resignation was particularly surprising because the principal at Barnard was someone who avoided conflict. When angry parents showed up at school, he was usually nowhere to be found. But he had the organizational authority that came with his position, and I suppose that many teachers had felt the effects of his decisions on their lives. And though they weren't happy with the administration, they complied out of fear or concern that their lives would be made miserable. It was hardly a motivating or professionally stimulating working environment.

But in my classroom I was happy. I loved the children and slowly began to feel more confident. I attended a staff development session for TMH teachers and met a professor from the University of Illinois at Urban-Champaign who was the speaker. He had such an exciting, optimistic view of teaching TMH boys and girls. I spent a great deal of time after that exploring and applying his "Try Another Way" theories in my classroom. I communicated directly with him. He was willing to help me and genuinely interested in my successes. Dr. Marc Gold went on to develop and share his theories and make a lasting impact on special education. Unfortunately, he died too young and too soon, at the age of 39, from Hodgkin's disease. From this experience, I learned to approach experts, to question them and talk with them about their ideas and perspectives. How approachable and willing so many of them are, and how intrigued to see their work applied by practitioners.

One of my applications of Gold's "Try Another Way" strategy was our jewelry making initiative. Using his approach, I designed the jewelry assembly tasks so that even my students could assemble jewelry with complicated patterns successfully. And the pieces turned out beautifully, so beautiful in fact, that we decided to sell them to the students at our school as presents for the upcoming Mother's Day. I figured that any funds earned could go to pay for our class field trips. Those 16 TMH kids made $750.00. I was so proud of them. Our jewelry was in such great demand throughout the school that we had to work overtime to keep up with the orders. Since it was near the end of the school year, I had the office open a separate bank account for my students so that the money wouldn't get "lost." We ended the year understandably proud of ourselves, with great plans for the next year.

Fate—well, the Chicago Public Schools bureaucracy intervened, however. Over the summer I received a letter informing me that they had made me a "supernumerary" teacher. That meant that my position had been closed out, and I had to find another one. After some checking, I found out that *my entire class* had been transferred to a nearby school for space reasons. Not wanting to give them up, I went to the new school, applied for my old position, and retained it. The new school, Whistler, was a pleasant one in a Black middle class neighborhood, and the faculty welcomed us with open arms. There were several special education rooms there, and they gave us a real classroom in a hall with other classrooms, not isolated as we had been in our old school. Now all I really had to do was get our $750.00 back, get it transferred from Barnard to Whistler. It made sense to me. The money was for these particular kids.

Much to my surprise, the Barnard principal refused to give the money to us. He claimed that they had made the money in his building so it should stay in his building! Our new principal, when I asked for his assistance, refused to get involved. We never saw that money again, and I always wondered how the Barnard principal could live with himself after taking money away from handicapped kids. The refusal of the Whistler principal to intervene also told me something about *him*. Now the score was one victory for me, one for the bureaucracy.

I continued to relish my classroom full of children and my association with Mrs. Bright, who also made the move. I kept bumping into the bureaucracy, however. I wanted to start a program for senior citizens in the neighborhood to come in and tutor the children. This would give them the one-on-one attention they so desperately needed. I was told that we couldn't do that because if a senior fell, we would get sued. I wanted to bring in tools and machines for home life skills training (e.g., irons and cooking equipment). I was told that I couldn't do that either because the children might hurt themselves. Don't rock the boat, don't make waves—that was the message. Don't try anything out of the ordinary, don't be creative, and don't be innovative. Conformity was the order of the day.

I taught that same class of children for five years, watching as my six-year-olds became preteens and the older ones went on to sheltered workshops. I think teaching the same children over a period of years, something tried as a reform today, has a good deal of merit. The teacher really gets to know the children, and how they learn, very well. My class had the feel of a family because we knew each other so well. That personalization and sense of community enhance learning. In contrast, I felt discouraged by the pressure to conform and strictly adhere to all the system and school rules. Some of the things I had hoped to do with my children were outside the bounds of their regulations—things that would have been good for them, but apparently not good for the bureaucracy. What I saw as bureaucrats going through the motions also discouraged me.

Take my evaluation, for example. Evaluation never crossed my mind through my first year at Whistler. One of the reasons it didn't was that the principal never appeared in my classroom. This was not a big surprise, as the Barnard principal never had either. I always received the highest rating from him at the end of each year. The Board of Education had a silly little form that had room for exactly one word about your performance (superior, excellent, fair or poor). Now here I was at Whistler. The principal had never seen one minute of my teaching (though my class always walked quietly in the hall, a major plus for any teacher). Now, on the last day of the school year, I received my paycheck and my rating from him, a demotion to "excellent."

I suppose that many people would be happy to be excellent. But I had previously received two "superiors" from the Barnard principal. I felt that this was a huge slap in the face, a real comedown. I arranged a meeting with principal. In his office I asked for an explanation of my rating. Much to my surprise, he couldn't give me one! He hemmed and hawed about how he never gave a "superior" to a first-year teacher at Whistler. I objected and reminded him that he had never come to my room, that I had received superior ratings at Barnard. I said it wasn't fair of him to have such a policy. Then, when I realized I was getting nowhere, I asked him specifically what I could do the following year to raise my rating. (I don't know why I thought ratings were so important, but then again, I do know. That one little word was the only feedback you received all year about how you were doing. That one little word. In a curious and even compelling way, it shaped your professional identity.) But the principal couldn't tell me one thing I could do to improve. There is no question that this incident marked the beginning of my continuing resistance to the idea of principal as the sole educational leader of the school. Most principals admit that they don't have the time to be leaders. Many don't have the knowledge base, either, but why do so few ever sense that teachers might provide the leadership that schools need?

But I tried to stand up for myself, as scary as it was for me. And it *was* frightening. *No one* in our school went up against our ex-Marine principal. He made all of the decisions, and we were supposed to conform. Typically we didn't question his authority. It probably wouldn't have occurred to me to do so if I had not been directly and negatively affected. Challenging the educational authorities in *any* school just wasn't done. It was almost like being in a child-parent relationship: if the teachers acted like good children, then the good principal left them alone. They labeled those "bad teachers" who chose to challenge the status quo "troublemakers." Then vindictive administrators made their professional lives miserable. They received the worst rooms, the toughest assignments. Often the harassment continued until the "troublemaker" had no choice but to leave that particular school, and perhaps even the system or the profession.

Such treatment had a chilling effect on the rest of us. The teachers' only real recourse was commiserating in the teachers' lounge. The norms of school life for adults didn't make for the kind of collegiality and motivation for which I was looking. The only way to get any feeling of professional power was, in fact, to *become* an administrator, something not every teacher aspires to. So if you did not want to become a principal, you had to make peace with the status quo. You retreated to your classroom, ignored the negativity of the complainers, and tried to derive as much satisfaction as possible *alone*, behind a closed door with the children.

Summer vacation is considered one of the perks of the teaching profession. A contradiction, isn't it? One of the highlights of teaching is not teaching. Summers off, however, offer a world of possibilities for teachers to travel, to study, to tend to their families, to pursue other interests. Ever since I had gone on a two-week tour in college to Germany, Switzerland, and Austria, I had wanderlust. After my first year teaching Lil, a fellow teacher and friend, and I went to Ireland. We explored the country, visited relatives we both had there, and literally fell in love with our common ancestral home. While our first visit was for only two weeks, we vowed to return the next year for the entire summer.

When that time arrived, Lil had other plans. Undeterred, I decided to follow through by myself. My grandmother's cousin, Jerry O'Brien, who I had visited the previous year, had a little cottage he would rent out. It happened to be vacant. He lived in Howth, a town outside

Dublin. He agreed to let me stay there for the summer. Jerry lived near my grandmother's brother and sister, that is, my great-uncle and aunt, and so I didn't feel too intimidated going off to Europe for the summer by myself because I would be near family, even if I had only met them once before. So I signed on for a ten-week charter to Ireland. I enrolled in a three-week international summer school session at Trinity College in Dublin, and I set off for a real summer adventure.

Living in Howth was magical. My grandmother, now dead, never had told me how absolutely beautiful Howth is. The cottage where she was born and raised was still home to her brother and sister, Uncle James and Aunt Francie. It sat literally atop a cliff overlooking the Irish Sea, an utterly beautiful view. The land at the top of the cliff was covered in heather. It was breathtaking. Uncle James and Aunt Francie never had married. They were full of stories of growing up, and they made me feel close to my now-deceased grandmother whom I had a special relationship with. It made me feel sad to think of her having to leave Ireland with her husband and children in the 1920s in search of a better life in America. She never saw her parents again. She saw her brother and sister only once after that, when thirty years later, she returned by ship to her home. I don't know if I could ever have left my family knowing I'd never see them again.

The Trinity College summer school was a fantastic experience. I met people from all over the world who were interested in this course which covered the breadth of Irish culture and history. We studied music and literature and drama and visited so many important sites. I fell in with a couple of teachers from New York City, and through them met one of the locals. His name was John Walsh. One thing led to another, as they say, and six months later I married Mr. Walsh. He came to the U.S. and was able to take a leave of absence from his electrician's job to study. He began to pursue a lifelong dream to get a college degree in engineering. My teaching job and his college schedule enabled us to spend summers in Ireland. All together, I spent eight summers in Ireland. It was an incredible way to get to know and love the birthplace of all four of my grandparents.

I had hoped that John would fall in love with the United States, so much that he would want to stay here. Unfortunately, that was not so. He was an only son who had inherited twenty-five acres of land. While not much by our farming standards, owning one's own land is critical to the Irish psyche. Neither one of us could make the choice to leave our home and family and country for good. After six years of marriage, he returned home. We keep in touch to this day.

Meanwhile, back at school, after five years at Whistler, I decided that it was time for some new challenges. I had since earned my Master's degree going to school at night and was now in fact qualified to teach children with learning disabilities. I began my search for, and found, a school that needed a learning disability teacher. At that time Chicago was under a faculty desegregation order. All I had to do was find another school that needed a white teacher. While sad to leave my TMH kids, the prospect of the unknown excited me. When he found out about my impending transfer, my Whistler principal had the nerve to call me in and ask me why I wasn't happy at his school. He wouldn't have understood even if I had told him. He didn't have a clue, and I decided not to waste one on him.

I began my experience as a learning disabilities teacher at Medgar Evers School, another school on Chicago's south side. This was another relatively new and physically attractive school in a Black, middle-class neighborhood, run by a woman principal. Several staff members who worked there when I arrived are still there, almost twenty years later. This is one of the truths of large urban school systems: superintendents and (and as they now call them, Chief Executive Officers) come and go (and in Chicago they mostly go), but not the front line professionals who provide our students commitment, continuity, and experience during their school years.

Just as had been the case at Barnard, the faculty at Evers immediately welcomed me into the fold. The position I filled, that of a resource teacher, meant that I pulled children with learning disabilities out of their regular classrooms for a certain part of their day. I would help remediate their learning (primarily reading) problems. I had a bright sunny corner room on the second floor. I tried to fill the footsteps of their revered former LD teacher who was the subject of continuing and constant raves.

School wide, the children were pleasant and interested in learning, and the discipline procedures in the school were solid. Since many children I saw were in the upper grades and had experienced years and years of failure, they had some motivation problems. I worked hard to apply everything I had learned in graduate school. I think that in the one year I was at Evers—though I was still learning how to be a good LD teacher—the kids and I made substantial progress. Outside my classroom door a different story was unfolding, however.

It turned out that the elegant and committed principal also was a dictator. Teachers cowered in fear of her, especially when she would go on a rampage against them, often in front of their children. She was a fanatic about test scores. She publicly posted the quarterly gains of students, so teachers could rank and compare themselves. I remember colleagues, particularly new teachers, coming to me in tears, having just been upbraided for something, with their children watching. The union rep (or delegate as they call them in Chicago), had a terrible time keeping up with the complaints and grievances against the principal.

She left me alone, for some reason. I always thought it was because I had asked to come to her school that she liked me. Actually, I had been remiss in not chatting with some of the teachers there before I transferred. If I had, I might not have made the change. I also think she left me alone because I had stood up to her relatively early after I arrived. For the first couple of weeks I was there, she canceled my classes blithely and used me as a substitute when teachers were absent. It's easy to cancel a LD resource program because you don't have to replace the person. The students, who should, by federal mandate, be served, just remain in their room. For the first few times I was asked to substitute, I didn't say anything. When it became a more continual practice, I went down to the principal's office and had my say. I reminded her how frequently I had been asked to cancel my program. I observed that I had not worked in the system for (then) six years only to come to Evers to be a day-to-day sub. I forget what she said, except that it must not have been too awful or I would have remembered. What I do know is that I didn't have to pull substitute duty more than once or twice the rest of the school year.

While being left alone by the principal was a good thing for me, teaching in an environment where so many lived in fear was demoralizing for everyone, including me. Here I was, in my third school in six years (one change precipitated by the Board of Education, one change by my own choice). I found that each school was worse than the last in terms of professional dignity and respect for the faculty. My first school, Barnard, had a laissez faire principal who avoided problems. The Barnard faculty didn't have any kind of shared professional culture. It was your typical, isolated behind-closed-doors kind of teaching practice. My second school, Whistler, had a benevolent dictator as principal, a man who followed the rules and expected conformity; for the most part, he got what he expected. Now at my third school, we had a dictator whose faculty cowered in fear for their jobs.

I was disillusioned. My expectations of what being a professional was all about were shattered. Where I had expected respect, the bureaucracy's demand was subservience. I had expected some control over the decisions affecting me and my students, the promise of the professor who urged me to finish school. Yet the bureaucracy demanded that I do what I was told to do, when I was told to do it, and how I was told to do it. Where I expected some kind of collegiality and sense of professional community with my co-workers, the bureaucracy demanded that we remain isolated and alone in our classrooms. Is this all there is? I asked myself. What had happened to the vision of professionalism my professor had shared with me? He had asked whether I wanted to be the one making the decisions or the one receiving them. I thought that I chose the latter. Did it really make any difference, though, that I had persisted and finished my degree? Did I really want to remain in a system that valued conformity and control over creativity and initiative? That valued bureaucrats and the bureaucracy over teaching and learning? The answer was no.

One might ask at this point, since I am now a teacher and a union activist, where was my union? The Chicago Teachers Union (CTU). A good question. I had little connection with it personally. I had not come from a union family, though my Irish grandfather was a union man who drove Chicago streetcars. My father was a salesman and my mother a homemaker, the mother of eight children. I was the eldest. I did not grow up hearing union talk. My only exposure to the union during those first six years of teaching was with the gym teacher at Barnard in my first year of teaching. She was a huge forbidding woman who approached me immediately and said, "You will join the union, won't you?" Of course, I did. We went on strike twice during my first six years of teaching, and that was my only other identification with my union—striking for better pay and benefits. In fact, I was on strike the first week of my teaching career. It never occurred to me, for example, to go to my union when the Barnard principal kept the hard-earned money my class had earned. I don't know what the union would have done. Other than taking my dues and informing me about picket lines, my union never reached out to me in any other ways. Not as a new teacher, or eventually, as an experienced teacher, as a professional. I didn't associate my questions about the professionalism of teaching with my union. Not then.

In what was the last spring before I left the Chicago Public Schools, I had taken a night class called "Writing for Publishing." I had always liked writing and wanted to explore my skills a little more. This class sounded perfect. Our assignment for the course was to get something published, a daunting feat it appeared to me. As I pondered what to write about, it occurred to me that I should stick with education because it was something I knew. I remembered a little newspaper clipping in the union's monthly newspaper describing a study that had just been completed on the subject of teacher stress. Roosevelt University and the CTU had conducted it jointly. I had the experience that it was not teaching that was stressful, but rather all the things that kept teachers from teaching. I called my union to get more information about this study.

I was referred to John Kotsakis who at the time was a field representative for the CTU and its liaison with Roosevelt University on the study. I was more than a little nervous as I walked into his office for the interview I had requested. It didn't help when—after he agreed to have the interview tape recorded—my batteries all fell out as I was lifting the tape recorder to his desk. So much for stress. The interview went well. Much to my surprise (and John's too, I would learn), they published my story about teacher stress. It was in one of the most prestigious of educational magazines, the *Phi Delta Kappan* journal.

To be honest, I had never read it or even heard about this journal. I just dutifully followed my writing instructor's advice. I sent the article to all the education magazines listed in *Writer's Market*, a book that appears annually with a listing of every publisher in the country. What surprised me even more, after they published the article, was a flood of mail, more than 100 letters. They came from all over the world, in response to my article. I returned to John's office with a complimentary copy of the magazine in hand, and thus began a friendship that lasted until his untimely death from heart disease in 1994.

In the fall of 1979, I resigned my position as a teacher with the Chicago Public Schools. I was disillusioned by the lack of professional respect and authority afforded to teachers in the system. I accepted a new position as a professional development specialist in a federally funded special education cooperative serving 55 school districts in the Chicago metropolitan area. This position required me to present workshops and other forms of professional development to teachers in these districts, on request, on issues concerning or about special education. This is where I learned how much I enjoyed teaching adults. At first glance I was awkward and tentative in my new responsibilities. I had my office (if you could call the space between the panel dividers an office). It included a telephone, and the use of a secretary who worked for two colleagues and me. I walked around the first couple of months in awe of the fact that I could go to the bathroom any time I wanted. I remember being self-conscious about my co-workers hearing me talk on the telephone. As a Chicago public school teacher, I didn't spend much time talking with other adults.

In this position I expanded my knowledge of educational systems. I learned how to research a variety of topics and present them in what I hoped were cogent and interesting ways. I learned how to work in a team setting as we pooled our knowledge and information for joint presentations. I became more poised, more confident in front of groups of my peers—no small accomplishment, for teachers can be the most critical of learners. At the beginning, I was devastated if even one evaluation at the conclusion of a session was negative. Soon I learned to judge myself. This was based not solely on what the participants liked, but whether I also felt that I had done my best in preparing and presenting the session.

Evaluation evolved from my being graded to a source of learning and revision for me. Still, having the teachers like you also was important in the work that we did. If teachers turned thumbs down at you districts wouldn't call you back, and that was a kiss of death. Administrators would be in trouble if the speaker they brought in bombed. They used to call our office and ask "What do you do that's **good**?" It didn't matter to them what the content of a presentation was or whether the teachers wanted or needed to know what we were offering. It just mattered that you would be "good," that you could keep teachers entertained. Again, I saw the paternalistic way that professional development was "done to" the teachers. For the administrators were usually men, and the teachers, usually women. Someone would pick up the phone and merely ask "What do you do that's good?" If the answers were satisfactory, a whole school or an entire district's professional development was taken care of under the federal mandate. And the teachers endured. No wonder that they were such a tough audience. No wonder they at least wanted to be entertained. But was this professionalism?

It became a daily question for me. Is having someone else make all the decisions for you, especially what you need to grow professionally, is that what being a professional is all about? For I learned quickly that the suburban districts we were serving had the same kind of command and control mentality that I had encountered in Chicago. It was a more subtle one, and on a more personal scale than the version favored by the big city school bureaucracy. And why were we teachers—including me in my first six professional years—so passive about it all? Why were we militants only when it came to issues of pay and security?

The writing and publishing of my article overlapped my transition from the Chicago Public Schools to the special education cooperative. I continued to have one foot in the city schools and one in the suburban schools. Many friends of mine who taught in the suburbs were taking classes toward their master's degrees and continued to advance on their pay scales as a consequence. The County Superintendent of Schools subsidized these classes. The County Superintendent's office was in charge of overseeing professional development and of teacher certification renewal. It also subsidized courses for teachers in cooperation with the teachers union that primarily represented suburban teachers, the Illinois Education Association.

I went to my friend John at the CTU and told him about this. I suggested that since Chicago was in Cook County, and since this office was subsidizing another union, perhaps our benevolent County Superintendent would oblige us, too. It took one telephone call from the then president of the CTU, Robert Healy, to convince Mr. County Superintendent to subsidize the course we were proposing. Thus began a part time job for me, one of those "That's a good idea, why don't you do it?" jobs that ended up influencing my professional career to this day. I organized and then started the Chicago Teachers Union Graduate Program. It was a busy time. Besides learning my professional development specialist position, and having my article published, I started working part time at the CTU. I also was embarking on a Ph.D. program.

Accidentally stumbled into a Ph.D. program is a more accurate rendition of history. I accompanied a friend who was looking into master' degree programs, and we were making stops at two or three universities in downtown Chicago. Our first stop was the University of Illinois at Chicago (UIC). While my friend was inquiring in the graduate office, I waited and looked over some literature in the waiting area. One piece described a new interdisciplinary Ph.D. program offered jointly by the Colleges of Education, Business, and Public Policy. Ever since I had completed my master's degree, I had toyed with the idea of going further. I always loved school. I remember laughing at myself, when one month after receiving my undergraduate degree I found myself back in school, taking courses toward my master's degree. A Ph.D. wasn't something that I had always aspired to, however.

Yet as I looked at that brochure, I saw the doctorate as another mountain to climb. Why not? Besides, few women had Ph.D.'s. Why would they? Not enough women entered leadership roles, even in education. Less than 3 percent of all school superintendents were women then, in a field that was predominantly female. The next thing I knew, I was standing next to my friend as we *both* completed our applications. Since UIC is a public university, the tuition was within my reach; all I had to do was get accepted.

I was going to school at UIC at the same time as the inception of the CTU Graduate Program. I was able to convince the College of Education at UIC to form a partnership with the CTU so that our courses could be offered for graduate credit. Being a student there also enabled me to find out which faculty members could relate to the real world of urban education and which could not. We wanted to offer compelling, relevant courses that would keep teachers coming back for more. Also, because the CTU operated this program, we knew we had to be rigorous and first-rate to overcome any criticisms about the union being in the education business.

Our program was an instant success, and no one was more surprised than I was. Every semester we had hundreds of union members, checkbooks in hand, down in the union office signing up for advanced course work. Some of them had never seen the inside of their union headquarters before, and the union staff had never seen so many members there all at once either. I remember, as I administered the program part-time from an empty secretary's desk, seeing the union president walk by. He would stare in amazement at the lines of his members coming to the union for a different kind of service. It was this experience that convinced me that teachers need their union to be as uncompromisingly excellent on the professional issues as it was on the bread and butter issues. Professional issues are just as much a part of working conditions as salaries and benefits are. Almost twenty years later, the CTU Graduate Program is still in business and going strong. The fact that it hasn't changed much over those years is another story. More on that later.

By 1982, I was ready to write my dissertation. Realizing that I couldn't juggle a full and part time job effectively, I decided that something had to go. That something was the full time job. Though friends and relatives thought I was crazy to give up secure full-time income, I knew that I needed to work on my research paper. I had enough money to scrape by. I also loved the union work and did not want to give it up. I had relished the challenges of my PDS job and had learned so much that would be valuable to me in the future. I also had come to realize that I liked change and challenge. So, with no current full time job and none waiting for me, I said good-bye to the Special Education Cooperative and hello to my typewriter. For I was determined not to be ABD, an acronym for "all but the dissertation." Seventy-five percent of Ph.D. candidates never finish their dissertations and complete the program. I swore I would not be one of them.

Chapter II.
The CTU Years, 1979-83:
Lessons From John Kotsakis

Thornton Wilder, the great American novelist, once had a character observe that we don't work on life; life works on us. There are incidents in one's life that tend to be crucial, that bend one's path irrevocably. For me one of the most important turned out to be that interview with the Chicago Teachers Union (CTU) Field Representative, John Kotsakis, the person I mentioned in Chapter One.

My union office had put me in touch with Kotsakis, the CTU liaison to a project done with Roosevelt University. It was that project that I needed to know more about as I wrote an article for a course that I could then seek to get published. I timidly asked him if I could interview him, and he graciously agreed. Now all I had to do was think of what to ask him. Yet the questions came easily and on the appointed day, tape recorder and index card full of questions in hand, I walked into John's office. It was neat but filled with piles of paper; the office walls were covered with labor-related posters and artwork. One huge picture dominated, and anyone who met with John in that office has to remember the vivid color and striking images of the fist of labor raised in protest. John was a handsome, slender, silver-haired, well-dressed man. He also turned out to be knowledgeable, articulate, and even visionary. I walked into that interview not sensing that it would forever change the direction of my professional life. Here is what we talked about...

Interview with John Kotsakis, CTU Field Representative
April 24, 1979
CTU Offices, Chicago, Illinois

Q: How did the idea for a Chicago Teachers Union Teacher Survey come about?

A: The union sponsored a conference on school discipline in 1976, and based on that it was determined that we would attempt to have a survey of teacher attitudes on discipline. This was apparently a concern. Yet it was very difficult to measure just how important an issue this was to teachers. Any poll of teachers had shown that discipline was the number one issue for them. Findings showed that discipline was the number one issue for them. We wanted to figure out that causal relationship. The conference committee and the ad hoc committee on discipline and as staff liaison to these committees, determined that we would prepare a questionnaire for our membership. We prepared and field-tested a sample survey in a couple of schools. I decided that if it were going to be a membership survey, it had to be as scientifically and statistically proper as it could be done. So I went to Roosevelt University and talked to Bob Koff and asked him if he could provide assistance. Bob asked if we had thought about working on the larger concerns of teachers. I had been focused on discipline. Was it really the number one concern of teachers? Even though they say it is, when people respond to surveys, there is always a hidden agenda in some responses. Koff suggested taking the idea and trying to expand on it. We then got the idea of basing the study on the Homes & Rahe Life Events Inventory, only we developed our own teaching events survey.

Q: And you based the CTU study on that?

A: I didn't do it myself. I worked with Bob and others from the UIC School of Public Health, and later Don Seeshon who was in charge of research analysis at Roosevelt. We doped out a survey, field tested it in *a couple of schools and at the next conference on discipline. On that basis we made a couple of changes and then the union voted to spend the money necessary to survey the entire membership. We decided to do that, rather than a sample survey because we didn't want to get into the cost of a statistical breakdown. We wanted to make sure that we got a good cross section of the membership. For that, you can go one of two ways, a blanket survey or a selective survey. So we sent it to all CTU members and hoped that the responses would be a cross section of the entire membership. And as it turned out, we got a really good 20-25 percent response rate. It was a good cross section of almost every group (male, female, racial, elementary schools, and high schools). It was a statistical cross section.*

Q: The results showed that 1/2 of the respondents checked physical illnesses and a quarter checked mental illnesses. Has there been any further research into who said yes and how they are managing?

A: There will be an analysis on the content of the narrative responses to provide some context clues for teacher health issues. Based on the surveys that I read, I would say that people are coping one of three ways. Obviously, those who are coping best are not putting it down, they're not having any problems, or whatever it is, it's not a major aspect of their work existence. First, those who are coping but not satisfactorily are going into withdrawal, withdrawing from activities in the school from association with their colleagues. Second, they are engaging in self-destructive mechanisms (drugs or alcoholism), and the third is that they give up.

Q: Is there any way to tell? Is the union keeping any information on those who are leaving, those who have burned out?

A: First, we don't know who leaves. I suppose you could find out if you read the Board reports. However, you're talking about a major research project to find everyone who resigns and say "Why did you resign?" It's a worthwhile one in terms of giving us some clues into what is bugging people. The school system does give them a form when they resign to say why, but they don't release that information to us. Yet there is no reason we couldn't survey people.

Q: So right now these people leaving are on their own to pursue other careers. The Board is not finding out why they're leaving?

A: No. Still, there is a clue. In New York City a couple of years ago, they had massive layoffs of about 4,000 teachers. Two years later they opened 2,000-2,500 positions and these 4,000 people were the first in line to get those positions. Of the 2,500 people whom they offered jobs, only 400-500 people wanted to come back. So the New York teacher' union did a survey of those people. What they found was that most people who didn't come back, didn't want to come back, though they were in lower paying positions. They gave reasons like "I'm treated like an adult on my present job. I didn't feel that way when I was a teacher." Or "I like to go to work some place where I feel safe" or "I like working in a place where it's clean." The point is, out of 2,500 people who had a chance to get a job, only 400 people wanted to come back.

Q: Your report also stated that more than half of the teachers wrote in additional stress events. What types of things did they write in?

A: I would say that most of them were repetitions. I went through about 300-500 responses. There was prevailing criticism of both local and central administrators, however. That was the main thing. There were also complaints about assignments, irrelevant paperwork, a lack of appreciation, and a lack of empathy from colleagues. I personally read every survey to get an idea of their concerns, and some people were in really dire straits when they responded to the survey.

Q: Do you think that many teachers are just locked into their jobs because they are not trained to do other things?

A: I think there are a couple of things that are operating here that give people a locked-in feeling. One is the fact that teachers, I think, have a very low idea of their own worth, of what they can do in the outside world. The skills they have in teaching can apply very well to many vocations. For example, management skills. There aren't many people who are in business as managers who have the responsibility of as many as 30-35 people. Teachers do that every day, in a very direct fashion. So first, they feel that they can't do something else, and second, they have a very overstated idea of how skillful other occupations are.

Q: The comment that you made about the prevailing unhappiness with administrators: how prevalent is that?

A: *Pervasive. I would say that most teachers are not satisfied with their school administrators.*

Q: And why is that? How can the Board of Education pick people who do not respond? I know that the HEW study that you listed as a reference said that the key to the school violence problem is firm and consistent school leadership. Yet, as you stated in your article, teachers are not getting support and administrators don't even admit that there are problems there. Why is that?

A: *I think that there are two things. One is that this school system, like several others in major urban settings-New York, Philadelphia, Detroit, is basically a military structure. These military structures are based on entrenched old bureaucracies and therefore are incapable of responding to any kind of crises or needed change. Secondly, the military, top-down, top-to-bottom chain of command, means that everything must be initiated from the top and then work down. So there is very little need for the local administrator to take any kind of initiative for anything simply because this initiative is not encouraged or simply discouraged. If there is a need—the administrator sees a need—he or she must work through the given channels. This is very discouraging if you want to start to do things. At the same time, they have given principals vast administrative prerogatives. Except those that the union has taken away from them through the contract. These prerogatives are fairly pervasive in terms of what the principal can do. The principal has total control of evaluation, has total control of determining the curriculum, selection of textbooks, heads of departments. They have* much power and authority. They use it but also feel abused, feel that they don't have any power. Yet school principals, by the rules of the Board of Education have tremendous authority, though it is not always used for educational purposes, but for political or bureaucratic ones.

Q: If discipline is such an issue, why doesn't the Board create some kind of discipline policy? Don't you think the lack of a consistent policy is a cause of teacher stress?

A: Yes, and the union has tried to force the Board into taking that kind of stand. We have done so through committees and that sort of thing, and yet there is no consistent policy. I think that the Board would rather pass that responsibility down to the principal. Yet the principal knows that if he acts in a certain way which causes any kind of controversy that the Board will not necessarily back him. So he will do nothing. The Board says you have all the power. The principal turns around and says, "But I don't have the authority to exercise it without knowing that I am going to be supported." So the ball keeps going back and forth. It would be easier simply to have rules. We've asked them to establish rules for what would be considered grounds for suspension or grounds for removal from the school. The Board of Education is not willing to do this. They use the argument that every school is different, but it's an argument for not doing anything.

Q: Is there any interest in getting to the root of so much of the misbehavior? Teachers today will tell you that the students that they are seeing today are no comparison to the ones they taught even five or ten years ago. They say that the children can't sit still in their seats. They have short attention spans, little desire to learn, and no concern if they're two, four, six years below level.

A: I don't know how to express this without being called a Neanderthal, but is it the school's responsibility to be constantly trying to find out what is that makes students tick? Or is it supposed to be the job of the school to set standards and have the students meet them? In other words, where is it that the individual must begin to accept some *responsibility for his or her own actions? Because the school system is just that, a system. Our schools take on or are given more responsibilities for students, yet are not given the resources with which to do it. Student health, sex education, nutrition...*

Q: Yet the teachers are getting it from all sides that they are doing something wrong, that it's their responsibility to make the student motivated.

A: This comes from many sources, the various school critics who have said that the responsibility for learning rests foursquare on the schoolteacher's failure to motivate the child. Their criticisms are not warranted, in some cases. Sometimes, however, they have value. For example, because we have said school attendance is mandatory, we must accept the child in the school. If you are going to accept those consequences, you have to accept the consequences for someone who doesn't want to be there. You have to be willing to address yourself to him or her. Well, I'm not sure that's exactly the intent of the mandatory attendance rules. We have gone a step further than the right to a common school education. Yet there are no resources for it. Obviously the public does not want to pay the cost for being responsible for these things.

Q: And what about the stress of student test scores? And test score comparisons with other districts?

*A: There has been a mounting demand, especially in the last ten years, to publish test scores and see who has the best scores and this form of accountability, is a source of much stress I am going to recommend a book for you by Dan Lortie called **Schoolteacher**, or maybe you've already read it. Lortie says that teachers enter the profession for various and sundry reasons just like anybody. Yet there are some major reasons why they do. Once they are in, there are some things that they expect, that if they don't get, it makes their jobs less palatable and less rewarding. One of the major things that teachers seek and need are "psychic rewards." These are things like a note from a parent saying* that "You have done wonderful things with my child." Or a little handkerchief at Christmastime. Or a student coming back and saying, "Thanks, if it wasn't for you, I wouldn't be here." These rewards are declining, getting fewer and fewer for teachers.

Q: Are the scores in Chicago the lowest that they have ever been?

A: No, in fact, the latest ones show a small increase. Still, that is to be expected because you see the kind of accountability system we have is designed to show improvement. You're a teacher, you know that Continuous Progress is not a reading system but a management system, by which you will record results. All they are interested in is managing data. If you design the Continuous Progress program a certain way, as they have done, you show there will be progress, a self-fulfilling prophesy. You say where you expect the child to be in three weeks, six weeks, whatever. Obviously, if you say that, you are going to do it and in any way you can. You'll move the children along at a pace which will be the result that you said you would.

Q: Do you see accountability getting stricter for teachers, that if they don't produce the Board of Education will get rid of them?

A: The Board isn't going to fire lots of teachers. They are incapable of firing lots of teachers. Most principals are incapable of visiting most of their staff. First, it's an impossible job. To know and understand what is going on among a staff of say, 30 teachers. The only time a principal visits is if he thinks someone is not doing the job, and by that time it's too late. Also, many principals do not understand the pedagogical issues. If I were the principal, how would I understand how to teach kindergarten children if I never taught kindergarten? I would be hard pressed to be able to look at the program, other than whether the teacher has control of the class, which is the most obvious thing. Why things are a certain way and how to improve them are two different things. In my job, I see the kinds of things the principal puts down for unsatisfactory ratings: lesson plan details, out-of-date bulletin boards, *reports are unclear or late, all kinds of things that have nothing to do with the pedagogical problem of how to get the ideas across.*

Q: I can understand this prevailing criticism of administrators. I've heard teachers say that they have gone to their administrators for help or advice. Then they tell them "You're the expert, you've got your degree in this, go look it up in your books!" Teachers are really left to fend for themselves when problems do come up.

A: *This is another aspect of what Lortie was talking about, that teachers feel that they are isolated. You see, we are not a profession, yet. We only think we are a profession. We are only professionals as private investigators, or similar workers, see themselves, or as in the expression, 'He did it in a very professional manner.'*

Q: Well, what is the definition of a profession?

A: *A profession is a group of people who have, one, a mutuality of concern and occupation; two, a code of ethics; and three, a means by which they can decide who becomes a member of their group. That's a profession, and we strike out on all counts. They may call us professionals, but back to the self image thing, teachers don't really feel like they are professionals. This is one of the reasons why unions have grown so much. The education associations said teachers were professional. Then after the Second World War, people started looking around and saying, "Yeah, I'm a professional, but look at the low salaries. The Board can fire me any time it wants. I don't have a thing to say about what goes on. Anytime it wants. The Board can put 40 kids in my classroom. They can tell me to teach science in an art class or mathematics in an auditorium. I'm not determining anything. I work with 30 other professionals, but we don't sit and plan anything. Sometimes I find textbooks in my room, sometimes I don't. I didn't select the people with whom I work. The principal selects the books, the kids in my class, the curriculum, and so on. So, where's the professional aspect? To add insult to injury, the Board says you are not only not a professional, but they will treat you like a factory worker on an assembly line. "You have the kids here, move them here.* "Everything is on pieces of paper. The whole reading approach is behavioral, meaning that knowledge is now broken down into little bits and pieces of information. A child learns the 'ph'sound, gets a check, learns what a noun is, he gets a check, and so on. Yet these are skills, and they have nothing to do with the composite, the whole. So we have turned away from the whole Gestalt notion which we never had much of in education anyway, and now we are Skinnerian.

Q: Is the union against, completely against, Chicago's Continuous Progress program?

A: I'll say this. The union doesn't have a policy in that sense. In fact, the Continuous Program, as envisioned by people, has some supporters. Some teachers like it, but they like it for different reasons. Some say, 'Well, we had to have this program because some of our colleagues weren't doing their jobs.' It goes back to blaming themselves. It won't produce the desired results. What it will produce is proof that people are doing their jobs without knowing whether or not they've done it.

Q: What about yourself? Why did you leave teaching and go this way instead of going into administration?

A: I don't believe in administration in education. It doesn't have any value. An administrator doesn't really serve any useful function in education, as far as I'm concerned. They serve a purpose in so far as having someone around who is responsible for certain management aspects of the school. Beyond that it isn't a very satisfying job. Unless, of course, you are a real educator. This means that your main goal is to provide leadership in the curriculum, helping the so-called professionals, so that they produce better results and feel better about their jobs. You act as like a chairperson of this large department of educators. What does an administrator do besides decide where the refrigerator goes, how many reams of paper go to what classroom? Unfortunately, and this is what really irks teachers, the lowest rung in the school, the lowest position in status in the school is that of a *classroom teacher. Every person who's in the classroom would like to get a job out of the classroom. In special education, or tutoring with five or six children. Assistant principal, consultant, administrative aide. Anything but classroom teaching.*

Q: And what about your decision to leave the classroom? Why did you decide to leave classroom teaching?

A: Well, because I thought I could do a better job here. I enjoyed teaching and got all of the psychic rewards I wanted. At the same time, my feelings were much the same as I see out there now. A sense of isolation. A lack of concern for other colleagues. A lack of group identity. What we should be doing, what this organization should be doing probably, and what teachers should be doing in general, is insisting that schools of education raise their standards way beyond what they are now. Then, when someone comes out of a school of education, they feel that they've really accomplished something. The people I went to school with were upward bound, middle-aged women who had spent their earlier lives being wives and mothers, and this was their first taste of education. Then there were men like myself who came from lower middle or working class backgrounds. This was, in the eyes of our families, a step up, to be a teacher. Those kinds of people, because they were upward bound, wanted to be teachers, had a clear idea of what it was to be a teacher. Those kinds of people, I think, do the best job. The best kind of teacher there is, the most successful, is not the most liberal teacher, or the most conservative or is the best educated. It is the person with the clearest idea of what he or she wants to do in the classroom and what they want to be as a teacher.

Q: Did the Board of Education acknowledge your stress study?
A: No.

Q. Will you be able to use any of the information you collected in collective bargaining?

A: Well that's one of the things that I've been disappointed about. We haven't really taken the study and tried to determine what we have to do. The study has, I think, some very broad policymaking implications, and because of that, the Board should be looking at it.

Q: Is the number of grievances increasing? What about the union's stress program developed because of this study?
A: Well, we've had about 1500 a year for the last five years, so they've remained basically the same. The union started the "Educator Support Program," a series of support groups for teachers under stress, but we have not gotten the kind of response to them that we expected. We are in the process of evaluating why. One reason, I suspect, is that many teachers do not want to admit that they need any kind of help. Two, I think that we have stressed the aspects of health and stress too much, rather than the practical aspects of how to manage.

Q: In going through the literature, you find that there is not much on teacher stress and burnout, is there?
A: It's all relatively new. I can say this, if the study did nothing else, we probably drew nationwide attention to the whole issue. There is a lot breaking out on this issue now, workshops, articles, and so on. The problem now is that most of what is written is cursory, overview stuff. The issue is how you really measure these things and what value you put on what people say. It's hard to measure comparisons. Is teaching more stressful than police work? It may be that if the person is confident and has a clear image of themselves you can do a job without the negative stress effects. Teachers may need to form among themselves a network of support. Teachers are not used to working together, doing anything together. I do know that the assembly line model we have is passe and that we can't afford to be isolated anymore.

I walked out of that interview a changed teacher, a changed person. Maybe radicalized is the better word. John was one of the brightest teachers I had ever met. He had clarified so much for me in such a short time together.

I look back on these questions and these answers now, some twenty years later. I am struck by how much of that interview has remained with me, has become part of my world view of the education system and the teaching profession. I am struck by how much of this thinking has influenced my own.

I suppose that I resonated with John's interpretations because they reflected my own experiences. He had been there. His analogies and examples became a frame of reference for me as I tried to make sense of the confusions and contradictions of teaching in a big city school system. I was coming to the conclusion that it wasn't *teaching* that was so stressful, but all of the things that keep you from being able to teach. These were things John had touched on: lack of administrative support on things like student discipline, lack of decision making about what is best for students, too many seemingly irrelevant demands and paperwork. Here, in this CTU study, my colleagues were providing evidence that I was not alone in my concerns and confusion. I realized that I, that *we*, were being forced to be bureaucrats in a bureaucracy rather than professionals in a profession. In alarming numbers, my cohorts across the city were reporting the stresses of their professional lives. Stress was taking a physical, and even mental, toll on the quality of their work and personal lives. They were describing their discouragement at the lack of status and respect afforded them by the system. They were describing their resulting disillusionment with the profession for which we had so much hope.

Here are some issues that struck me from that interview:

Command and control hierarchy. John's command and control analogy made perfect sense to me, though it had never occurred to me before. Nothing of significance happened in a school that didn't come from a directive from "downtown." Who downtown was and why "they" decided was a mystery to us. Things were never explained to the people in the trenches. All we were told was to just do it. With whatever latitude they had, or thought they had, or suggested to us they had, principals decided in the same mysterious way.

Accountability. The issue of discipline is a perfect example of the anonymity and lack of accountability in a huge bureaucracy. As John said, while the central office would not take a stand on a system-wide discipline policy, neither would it support local administrators for taking a stand. As a result, nothing was done. So we teachers and support personnel were left holding the bag, so to speak. Funny enough though, nobody at the top or middle of the hierarchy, no one in management could be blamed. It reminded me of what political scientist Hannah Arendt once said. She described bureaucracy as "being ruled by Nobody. In a fully developed bureaucracy," she stated, "there is nobody left with whom one could argue, to whom one can present grievances, on whom the pressures of power can be asserted." I think Chicago teachers felt the same way concerning student discipline and many other pressing issues.

Blame the teachers. This was a very disturbing theme in my interview with John. Disturbing, and painfully true. It was the teachers, the lowest in the pecking order (other than the students) who so often took the blame in the media, in the community. Blame for not being able to control unruly and unmotivated kids, and blame for the resulting low student achievement. And, it seemed to me, blame for finally giving in to the system and giving up on their dreams of really making a difference.

Low self esteem. Once you have given up, however, you feel that you have let yourself down, not to mention your students. The feelings that teachers reported—the lack of professional respect and dignity; the lack of input; the fear of arbitrary and capricious administrators, were most distressing. Under these circumstances how could anyone be expected to convey the necessary strength and self respect needed to teach with confidence? Or with the joy we thought we would be teaching with when we dreamed about being teachers?

The notion of psychic rewards. The idea of psychic rewards intrigued me. Could not getting these rewards contribute to teacher stress? It made sense because we know teachers don't go into the profession to get rich. They go into teaching for a myriad of altruistic reasons. Anyone who has ever received one of those letters that John spoke of, a note of gratitude from a parent or student, knows that *just one* can make your entire school year worthwhile. How could the psychic rewards be increased, I wondered?

The role of the principal. I totally agreed with John's assessment of the role of the principal. The idea of principal as educational leader in the school continues to contradict any sense I have of teaching as a profession. Why can't the teachers be the leaders? The principal-as-educational-leader idea infers that there can be only one leader, usually the male principal, and the female teachers are the followers, as if the females needed to be "led." It is truly impossible for a principal, trained to teach in one field or developmental level, to evaluate and provide constructive support to twenty or thirty, or in high schools, over one hundred faculty members. Many teachers have far greater experience, knowledge, and expertise in their fields. It's not that no one needs them at all in a school. But as managers providing the logistical support and assistance to the teachers so that they can do what they are good at. This relationship is akin to a hospital administrator's relationship to doctors. Why aren't teachers seen as leaders? Even in their own profession?

Teaching as a profession. Before that day with John, it never occurred to me to question whether teaching was a profession. I had always been told it was a profession, had always thought of it as one. Yet when measured against the criteria for one, a body of knowledge of practice, control of the entry process, discretion in decision making, and a code of ethics, we fell far short. What would we need to do in education for teaching to earn this distinction?

Collegiality. One of the things we would need is a culture of working together. So far the only thing I had observed teachers doing together was commiserating about their collective situation. I thought of how doctors worked with their colleagues. They collaborated on patient care (instead of trying things alone in the classroom). They used discretion in applying the latest research to their practice while taking each patient's individual needs into account (instead of being told what to do, when to do it, and how to do it). They had accepted and relied upon a body of knowledge (instead of the "anything goes" approach). It sounded so foreign to me, but so exciting. What would teacher collegiality look like, feel like?

The union's role in professional issues. This interview was the first time I had ever turned to my union for anything. I had, by this time, been involved in two strikes and had a vague notion that the union stood for enforcing our contract and striking for better working conditions. The union had never reached out to **me** on any issue. Was teacher stress a union issue? A working condition? Was teacher professionalism a union issue? Was it a working condition? Did the union have a role in teacher professionalism? Were the issues it stood for moving us in any way from the role of bureaucrats, to professionals? I had never associated teacher unionism and teacher professionalism before, but the possible association astounded me with its logic. We were a union of professionals. Could those two terms—union and professional—be mutually *inclusive*?

John had been gracious enough to allow me access to the CTU stress survey responses so that I could do a content analysis. I followed up on this opportunity. As John had told me, this survey had been developed to be consistent with the methodology employed by two researchers, Holmes and Rahe. Holmes and Rahe had established, through medical and psychological research, that certain life events are associated with the onset of stress and illness. In the CTU/Roosevelt study, 36 teaching events were presented and they asked teachers to rank the events in terms of their relative degree of stressfulness. I was curious about those 36 events, because I was beginning to question whether stress was the issue here. I had a vague feeling that perhaps something else was going on here. The survey also provided opportunity for narrative comments from teachers by requesting teachers to list any additional event they felt should be listed. I ended up doing a content analysis of a random sample of 700 of the five thousand returned questionnaires.

Of the 700 teachers whose surveys I studied, 60 percent took advantage of the opportunity to respond and elaborate on work related stressors. I found that an astounding 81 percent of their comments attributed work stress to organizational factors, primarily "the system" or "the principal." The remaining 19 percent to issues like colleagues (6 percent), students (5 percent), safety (4 percent), and parents (4 percent). I found substantial dissatisfaction with the intrusion of bureaucratic authority in three major areas: 1) unrealistic expectations from the Board of Education; 2) inconsistent policies; and 3) lack of support.

The major concern on expectations had to do primarily with what they described as insurmountable, irrelevant and unrealistic paperwork that they saw as having nothing to do with helping students. "So much teaching has become an accidental by-product of paperwork," wrote one teacher, illustrating the problem. "Just to give you an idea of the absurdities that hinder my teaching, there is lunch money, picture money, fundraising money, attendance forms, behavior charts, criterion referenced tests, racial spot maps, bilingual surveys, foster home reports, individualized education plans...a crush of non-teaching responsibilities."

Teachers criticized both policies and policymaking processes. They reported being outside the decision making processes and not being given adequate information with which to understand and incorporate the rationale behind policies. There were confusing communications, constantly changing rules and regulations, and even conflicting directives. They expressed particular concern about policies on untested programs, imposed on them with little consideration of their needs in carrying them out. "We have to carry out programs with little introduction or explanation, and no idea how long it will continue before they start a new program," said one respondent.

Professional support to the teachers whose responses I studied seemed to mean three things: adequate resources, relevant help with work-related problems, and professional respect. These teachers repeatedly described their rooms and schools as cold, poorly lit, and uncomfortable, even dangerous. A lack of funds, books, material was commonplace. Disillusionment develops when the system does not provide the essentials to do what the system gives lip service to as the most important work in the school. "There is a lack of concern with the employees and with problems found on the job," stated one teacher concerned about this issue. "There is no rapport. The principal is not interested in my problems and seems oblivious to teacher needs. When you have a problem, you are patted on the head and told to handle it."

Not surprisingly after what John had said, these teachers questioned the competence of the principal frequently. They criticized administrative incapacity and pettiness, inadequate and weak leadership, unqualified principals with little or no classroom experience, and arbitrary and capricious treatment. Did these statements reflect a conflict between what teachers feel a principal **should** be doing to meet professional needs, and what the principal **has** to do in terms of organizational priorities? While they reported wanting decisive, assertive leaders who would act quickly and decisively, they also sounded wary of decision-making concentrated in the hands of one person. Another professional-bureaucracy conflict? And why were concerns and complaints about principals so rampant? Were teachers stressed out by the use and abuse of power in their work relationships?

One teacher described "the feeling of pressure from the principal in all ways in trying to carry out programs the principal needs to get promoted. We experience harassment at faculty meetings, for example, where the principal insults the faculty and lays blame for all of the school's ills on us." Another teacher wrote, "There is a disregard for human dignity, for the rights of each individual. Principals are gods you must obey." Did principals know how to use positive motivation? Need schools operate out of fear?" Were these teachers describing stress or power? Stressfulness or powerlessness?

Other related issues concerned the use and abuse of a principal's limited power in the system, poor communication, non-recognition of work efforts, lack of encouragement. "There is a remote, impersonal, almost hostile attitude of the principal which causes polarization of the faculty instead of unity," stated one angry respondent. "There is a lack of respect for teacher judgment. Any communication is negative never positive. Any dealings with the principal or district administrators are most stressful, as you are treated always as a child, never with respect or dignity."

What are these administrators expressing to teachers by this lack of recognition and respect? And why do teachers care so much what administrators think about them? Are these teachers' perceptions accurate? And how was the power dependence theory operating here, I wondered? Are some principal behaviors reported here a function of the principal's own power status in the system? Is the principal using whatever power leverage is available to survive in the system? The principal, a former teacher, now is in a position of different priorities and influence over teachers. What effect did this have on teachers' perceptions of a principal's use of power, I wondered?

These comments confirmed what Lortie found. Teachers achieve their most fundamental rewards in their work with students, yet more teachers listed aspects of professional autonomy than working with children (e.g., "Doing what I want in my classroom"; "Knowing what is expected of me and doing it without interference"; "Using my own initiative.") These statements seemed to be statements of power and autonomy, not stress. They were saying that they needed the autonomy to make decisions in the classroom and needed to be able to teach with relative freedom from organizational constraints. It seemed to me that it was the principal, the embodiment of the system for the teacher, who had the unique capacity to restrain or unleash feelings of professional power in teachers. Lortie had also made the connection between rewards and power when he described teachers influencing the flow of rewards. I found it very significant, then, that when teachers in the CTU survey were asked about work-related stress, they identified the system and the principal as their major obstacles to obtaining and achieving the rewards of the job.

Stress or powerlessness? The question of what was really happening here with this issue of teacher stress kept at me. Even the phrase itself bothered me, because the word stress inferred that something inherent in the work itself was negative, which I knew wasn't true. New frames of reference were presented to me by John, and others whose work I began reading. I continued to wonder whether teacher stress wasn't a misnomer for something else. Were we focusing on the symptoms but not the underlying disease? For as I began to examine the surveys that John shared with me, I began sensing another phenomenon at work. This phenomenon also resonated with my own teachering experience. Over and over again I heard it: a lack of respect, a lack of influence, a lack of control over one's work life. Finally, when I read one teacher's insightful comments, they confirmed for me that this wasn't an issue of stress at all. This teacher wrote, "I find the most stressful factor in my work to be the feeling, and the fact, of powerlessness in the bureaucracy. There is a total lack of being part of the democratic process. We teachers are at the mercy of petty bureaucrats whose power is paper pushing and who have lost sight of the fact that we must *create* with students." The issue here was not stress, I finally realized. It was the two-sided coin of power and powerlessness. This was the intolerable burden we carried as teachers, alone and together. I had found the focus for my inquiry, and for my activism.

Chapter III.
The Ph.D. Years, 1980-83:
Power and Powerlessness in Teaching

I embarked on the feared and dreaded doctoral dissertation process. Unlike my "Writing for Publishing" assignment, I now knew exactly what I wanted to explore. The topic, teacher power and powerlessness, far from being an esoteric and theoretical one, became a burning, real-life issue for me then, and for years to come…

"Teaching was not my first job," kindergarten teacher Flo Donnels told me. Donnels, a spunky, single woman in her late fifties had a master's degree and taught on the city's South side. She had responded to my dissertation survey on teacher power and reported having very little of it. She was one of the teachers who, along with their principals, had agreed to be interviewed about their thoughts on teacher power and powerlessness.

Flo continued, *"I previously worked in industry. I thought of teaching as a profession then. Now I look at it as a civil service job. There is no respect like a doctor or a lawyer. Teachers are not allowed to make their own decisions. I thought I would have the power to teach, to be creative, to question the suitability of programs. We are trying to fit the child into the program. I am helpless to do what I know would help them. I have to do what I'm told to do…I can't help the children survive the system. No more individual help—it's mass teaching. I'll do it because I have to do it, but it hurts me. I've even thought of forgetting it. Maybe it's me, but I'm trying to give it some more time...*

"What gives me professional power? When I see the growth of children, the change in behaviors. When I know I've had an impact on someone's life. When you effect a change in a child's life. It's seeing adults, professionals, come back to see me. When you see some become upwardly mobile. In a community like this—broken down, poverty-stricken—many never get to move out...

"At this time, in this school, I have felt a sense of powerlessness," Flo continued. *"Morale is very low, professional rapport, poor. I have a philosophy that it's the teachers who should run the school. Principals can only do so much, but what they have to do is negative. If a staff pulls together to do what is good professionally, if everyone is doing what they are supposed to do, what can the principal say? When you negate your responsibilities, you're giving the principal the power to control you."*

In his now famous book about teaching, **Schoolteacher** (the book that John had so strongly recommended to me), sociologist Dan Lortie talked about power. He pointed out that the very fact of employee status denotes subordination and that teachers were, in fact, officially employees without powers of governance. He described how organizational control over teachers is achieved by what he termed "subtle mechanisms": the way teachers are selected, their socialization, and the standard operating procedures, (e.g., the bell schedules, the signing in and out procedures, the tight control of limited supplies). Lortie also raised the politically incorrect issue of the predominance of females in the teaching profession and the implication of the feminization of teaching. "We have yet to see," he said, "whether any occupation predominantly female in composition can or will achieve clear title to the honorific designation of 'profession'. It appears that considerable militancy and knowledge-building must occur if teachers are to get the status associated with high prestige professions." These statements, written in 1969 still pertain as I write today, 30 years later.

Another well-known sociologist, Amatai Etzioni, had even coined an apt phrase to describe professionals who work in bureaucracies—the "semi-professional". When you think about it, the potential for conflict is clear. Where bureaucracies stress rules, conformity and efficiency, professions stress a knowledge base, professional discretion and the needs of the client. Etzioni characterized semi-professions as having no specialized body of knowledge. They have little or no autonomy. They are controlled by a hierarchy. Most of the occupation is female. Most discouraging, the primary task (i.e., the work itself) is *devalued* as one advances in one's career.

These characteristics described my experience of teaching exactly. Real professions lay claim to a knowledge base, with professional autonomy and the primary tasks retaining high status. We teachers, however, are at the whim of the latest educational fad. They tell us what-to-do and when-to-do-it, and how to do it. The reality is, the farther you get from the teaching act, the more status, respect and remuneration you'll have. We hear of eminent doctors and eminent researchers all the time, but when was the last time you heard of an eminent teacher? What happens to a profession, I wondered, when its primary task actually *loses* prestige and those who become administrators are most rewarded and most associated with power? What effect can this have on those practicing this primary task when the profession itself rewards those who *leave* the classroom?

Not only do we professionals working in bureaucracies experience dual, potentially contradictory, roles. Having a weak profession (or "semi-profession") actually *compounds* the problem. They train us with the understanding that teaching is a profession. We assume that we can exercise the authority that we believe is inherent in our role. Then we arrive at the schoolhouse, and the bureaucracy won't let us *use* that authority. Is our profession's weakness *because* of its being predominantly female? What effect does this have on our power in the school, and in the profession itself? All the status, respect and power of the teaching profession appear to be concentrated in the hands of a few, predominantly male administrators. At the time I was working on my dissertation, only 3 percent of school superintendents were women, in a profession where nearly 80 percent of teachers are women.

I kept coming back to the role of the (usually male) principal. The principal represents the organizational, bureaucratic authority over teachers. This relationship, I thought, was the point where the two bases of power, the professional and the bureaucratic, converge and perhaps collide. Could this explain why teachers in the CTU survey reported such "pervasive" criticism of their principals? Why did it feel like principals had all of the power and teachers had none?

Eric John was the principal of Flo Donnel's school. I had identified three teachers reporting high, medium and low levels of professional power and their principals. I then requested interviews trying to get a closer, more detailed look at this phenomenon. Donnels had reported low professional power. Johns, her principal, was in his mid-thirties. He stated that he held five master' degrees and two Ph.D.'s. John's office was a stark room with little evidence of the job, no bookshelves, nothing on the walls. He responded casually, almost flippantly to the interview questions.

"Teachers have power within the constraints of the Board's curriculum. Any teacher can motivate some individuals. It all depends on the match between one's abilities and one's situation. The problem is teacher preparation, courses in theory. After kindergarten and first grade, we put people in boxes. Do we teach teachers divergent thinking? Teachers are not trained in creative thinking. The Board's curriculum stifles it.

"For the most part, I treat teachers with respect. I'm human, too. Sometimes I get mad. I came here three years ago to a very negative attitude. I've been playing the clean-things-up role after inefficient administrators who let teachers do anything they want. People whose vested interests were threatened are now beginning to understand. There is two way communication. They bring a problem to me and we work on solutions. Teachers are satisfied with my level of administrative support. I

support them in the following areas: supplies and materials, curricular assistance, discipline, and dealing with parents. It's also supporting teachers in front of parents and students. I also send out weekly bulletins or 'words from on high'. Teacher stress comes from the inability of teachers in a building to support each other and share resources."

Comparison of these two responses is illuminating. An older teacher who sees a punitive and authoritarian administrative style as causing poor morale and resentment. A young principal who feels that he *does* share power, but that he is in a situation where he has to do much "cleaning up." Both professionals recognized poor morale and a lack of faculty support of each other as real problems, but attributed different causes and proposed different solutions. Ms. Donnels also spoke of racial favoritism (she was Black, her principal was white). She reported a grave lack of respect which she felt also contributed to resentment and a lack of unity. Dr. Johns spoke of sending memos from "on high" and the lack of teacher creativity and divergent thinking, both inferring a kind of superiority or condescension which could have come across to teachers.

There were age, race, gender *and* power differences at work here. These, combined with favoritism and a punitive, authoritarian administrative style seemed to account for a good deal of Ms. Donnel' feelings of professional powerlessness. She seemed to love teaching and working with her students and, despite the bureaucratic constraints, found ways to give her students what she felt they needed. Several of her statements were contradictory, however (e.g., comments that teachers didn't have to let the principal have power over them, that she was helpless in light of bureaucratic demands). These suggested a struggle to reconcile the conflicts she faced. The school-wide strife and disharmony also seemed to be taking its toll. Yet it was the perceived inadequacies in administrative support and leadership which predominated and compounded, if not caused, her sense of powerlessness. Classroom power seemed to be necessary, but not sufficient for this teacher's sense of professional power. Was this true for all teachers?

My studies brought me to power-dependence theory. Developed by a researcher named Blau, the theory states that the amounts of dependence and interdependence that people have in a relationship reflects the stakes that each has in the relationship. Each person's power is determined by the other person's dependence on him or her, and the other person's value of the outcomes. In other words, the greater your dependence on someone, the greater that the power that someone has in the relationship. This idea of interdependence between principal and teacher intrigued me. We needed each other. We both wanted to see successful teaching and learning in our schools, didn't we? Why then, I wondered, didn't it *feel* like interdependence? Instead, it felt like powerlessness. Why was the balance of power so lopsided when, to make our schools work, the principal needed the teachers just as much as the teachers needed the principal? This relationship, I started to believe, symbolized the conflict between the bureaucracy and the profession, between conformity and autonomy, between the powerful and the powerless, and, perhaps, between male and female.

Other researchers described how those with power develop and maintain the acquiescence of the powerless by preventing certain issues and actors from gaining access to the decision making processes. One's view of power can be altered as an adaptive response to the use of power. Continual defeat of those without power leads to their refusal to challenge the powerful due to their expected response. Then, over time, this withdrawal of the powerless will remain unchanged without the powerful ever having to exercise their power. Even the *potential* for power is enough to alter behavior.

I could relate to this from my experience with the principals with whom I had worked. Just the possibility that the principal could arbitrarily punish teachers (e.g., scream at us in front of our students, give us the least desirable teaching assignments) was enough to keep most of us in line. We certainly had no access to the decision making processes. We used to joke that shared decision making in education means that the administrators make the decisions and share them with the teachers. Is *that* professionalism?

What was the difference between those who did and did not feel powerful, I wondered? I began to think of professional power as some kind of continuum. This led me to develop a "Professional Power Survey," which became the research instrument for collecting the data for my dissertation. I had to do several kinds of statistical analysis to ensure that the survey was a reliable and valid indicator of professional power. I also had to show that the four types of power included (classroom, school, system and power derived from the teacher-principal relationship), represented four distinct scoring categories. The survey also was designed to yield a composite score which was also confirmed to be a predictor of power and powerlessness.

With the help of then-CTU President Robert Healy, I was able to select a random sample of 300 CTU members working in elementary schools. The surveys were sent to the homes of these teachers, with a cover letter from Mr. Healy asking for the teacher' support and participation in the project. This assistance from the president of the teachers' union was almost certainly responsible for the substantial response rate that I received.

I wanted to find teachers at several points on my hypothetical power continuum, and interview them if I could. I had to do another statistical procedure to enable me to randomly select a smaller, but a representative group of teachers reporting high, medium and low levels of professional power. I ended up interviewing nine teachers, three each at the high, medium and low end of the continuum, and their principals, including Flo Donnels and Eric John. I was deeply appreciative of all the time and assistance these teachers and principals gave me. Their stories have remained with me on my own professional journey in teaching and have helped shape my thinking about the nature of school work.

The responses to the survey itself were more positive than I had expected, and in fact, contradicted the teacher' own reports of professional power. In the four categories of professional power, they generally agreed to having classroom power (with a mean score of 1.8 on a five-point scale, where one was strongly agree and 5 was strongly disagree). They were neutral on having any school power (with a mean of 2.9), neutral on power derived form the teacher-principal relationship (a mean of 2.9), negative on having any system power (mean of 3.6), and they were neutral on their overall professional power composite scores (mean of 2.8). That the highest agreement came in classroom, or expert, power, didn't surprise me. Yet even in this one realm where teachers reported experiencing power, the conflict between professional autonomy and bureaucratic control emerged.

The school power responses were confusing. On the one hand, teachers agreed to such statements as having the authority to set standards of behavior, having an important role in school policymaking and having the ability to discuss problems without fear. But then they disagreed with such statements as teacher input influencing the principal, teacher input being invited and listened to and having control over their working conditions. Forty-seven percent agreed that teachers had an important role in policy making and forty-six percent agreed that teachers were involved in joint decision making. How could an even greater percentage disagree that teacher input was invited and listened to, I wondered? These statements gave me lots of questions to raise in the interviews. Remember,overall teachers in my study overall reported being neutral on having any school power at all.

The teacher-principal relationship statements raised even more questions and contradictions. The vast majority reported satisfaction with administrative support, with the principal's leadership of the school and with the level of respect from the principal. Yet a majority were dissatisfied with teacher-principal communication, the principal's valuing and encouraging teacher judgment, and with sharing power with the staff. These contradictions left many questions to be explored as the teachers also reported being neutral on having any power deriving from the teacher principal relationship.

I was not surprised by the finding that the teachers reported having no power in the overall system (e.g., satisfaction with system leadership, the ability to teach without interference, rules and regulations enhancing professional power). But their answers here, too, seemed inconsistent with their other responses, such as their reported levels of job satisfaction and intention to remain in teaching. Were they suggesting that system power was not essential to one's satisfaction with teaching? Did teachers even *want* power in the system? I embarked on personal interviews to try to learn more.

Mary Sawyer was a single, vibrant teacher in her thirties, who taught fifth grade in a school on the near north side of Chicago. She scored in the high professional power range, describing her level of job satisfaction, level of commitment to teaching and intention to remain in teaching to be high.

"I consider teaching a profession," she said. *"A strong one, because it's part of you, part of your personality to motivate children to reach their capacities. When I came into teaching, I wanted to be able to control my classroom with love. I wanted my students to know that I was in control of what was going on. I put myself into it. I was a very strong disciplinarian. Now, after 13 years, I'm not nearly as tight. I am more lenient, more relaxed. As I grew in the profession, I didn't need those rigid things. It becomes natural after a while.*

"I experience professional power when I am making decisions about a child passing, decisions in grade level faculty meetings. Powerless? Usually in situations with a difficult parent, if I've tried to do everything and still get no cooperation. I like this school and we have much power in our grade level, quite a bit of power and say-so. It's a small school. Children give respect.

"I would rate the teacher-principal relationship as only fair. I don't know why. There are many things around here that are kind of loose. This relationship affects the sense of power a great deal. Some teachers have power to do certain things. Others do not. Many teachers feel threatened by him, but I don't need him and his support...With the

*faculty he has lots of power and he uses it as fairly as he can. I hear teachers complaining about him not being the backbone. He does not use rewards or punishments... Teacher power? She has it if she exerts it...There is not much interference from the principal. When I decide to do something, I'll do it, for the children...Teachers should control the work and not let the work control them. In the classroom, teachers need good control but must have patience, kindness and understanding of students' problems. As far as being rewarded, some people need rewards. I don't need them...I found out that **you** make the situation."*

Mary's principal, Carl Gray, gave a great deal of time to his interview. He answered my questions thoughtfully and with some soul-searching.

I certainly consider teaching a profession. It doesn't have the prestige of law and other professions. You'll never get rich in this profession. It appears we're all having fewer and fewer decisions to make today. Board mandates have taken a lot away from us. Teachers have lost a great deal of authority, but generally, they have authority over activities benefitting students. Otherwise, the system would have collapsed. Teachers have power in the sense that no one is watching over them all of the time. There is a great deal of trust in education. I don't know what all they are doing unless it's outlandish. I certainly feel that teachers can use their initiative. They are free to do it here. All they have to do is ask for things.

"*I try to encourage professional growth, but I don't do as much as I would like to do. Sharing power? Not really. I make many decisions that I could share with them but it takes too much time. I don't do what I intended to do as a principal. There is not a whole lot of time to meet. It's very difficult...I invite and listen to faculty input. Most would say 'He tries, but really doesn't do enough'. I'm frustrated because I don't feel that I do enough for them...Teacher submissiveness? I think most of them are real pussycats and will do what they're told. There is a certain element of apathy. But you would not have a school if you had ten people who always questioned things.*"

There was reasonably strong agreement between this teacher's survey responses and her principal's responses, which perhaps partially explains her reported high levels of professional power. Mary had a belief in herself and her ability to handle things, despite what she described as a lack of cohesiveness on the faculty, and a less than perfect administrator. She perceived the principal as trying to be fair, trying to provide support and trying to seek teacher input. If anything, Mary seemed to experience more power than the principal believed teachers had. Perhaps her self confidence, and her belief that she didn't need the principal and his support, were the difference between power and powerlessness for her.

Overall, teachers who reported high levels of professional power all cited good-to- fair relationships with their principals. They also reported a sort of distancing mechanism, or lack of dependency on the principal. Good relations or lack of support were not critical to their sense of effectiveness or power. Even when this relationship was only fair, if the teachers perceived that the principal tried to be fair and tried to show respect for the teachers, they reported more professional power. All of the high-powered teachers reported being left alone by the principal. This suggested that being able to teach without interference from the principal is important for a teacher's sense of power. It could also be that such non-interference is perceived by these teachers as a statement of the principal's confidence in their judgment and their ability to do their jobs.

A sense of mutual respect also emerged from these interviews with teachers reporting high professional power, and their principals. The medium and low power teachers did not report this quality of respect, suggesting that it is important, perhaps essential for the experience of professional power. Teachers reporting low levels of professional power on the other hand, questioned even the extent of their classroom power. They all reported negative relationships with their principals, characterized by coercive, punitive uses of administrative power, little support or respect, and poor morale. These teachers claimed less classroom power than any of the other groups of teachers. They also reported little or no school or system power. Yet it was the teacher-principal relationship that received the most criticism and the most emphatic responses. Their lowest survey scores were on this relationship, whereas the high and medium powered teachers reported their lowest scores in the system power category. This relationship appeared to color all other aspects of the work lives of teachers reporting low power. This confirmed for me the extreme importance of this relationship in the empowerment of teachers.

Not all teachers blamed their principals. The group of teachers that specifically identified the principal as a major contributor to their feelings of powerless is the group that reported autocratic, punitive and manipulative principals. So while this relationship represents the convergence of professional and bureaucratic tensions and demands, there might not be an inherent conflict in the relationship per se. If true, then *nearly all* teachers would have reported such conflict. Conflict seemed least when there was open communication, when the principal treated teachers with respect, considered teacher needs when making decisions, and explained such decisions. Even unpopular decisions seemed to be accepted when they received an explanation for such action. Such a democratic leadership style, based on dignity and respect, appeared to foster teacher' professional power, while the autocratic, punitive style actively discouraged its growth. The laissez faire leadership style also seemed to have a detrimental effect on professional power, as teachers reported that it connoted apathy and a lack of concern.

The high-powered teachers seemed to be saying that the greater their experience of professional autonomy, respect, administrative support, and school-level influence, the greater their overall sense of power. Yet these elements, the key differences between the teachers reporting high and low power, were all controlled, to some extent, by the principal. This might have been acceptable if classroom (or expert) power was enough to provide a feeling of professional power in teaching. But all these teachers told me that it was not. Classroom power was necessary, but not sufficient. They also needed to feel powerful at the school level—power derived from the teacher-principal relationship—and feel at least neutral on system power.

At the time of my power study, I drew several conclusions about what it takes to empower teachers: respect, influence, support and autonomy. These didn't appear to cost much money, in theory. Yet I felt that, in reality, the cost might be more than principals, more than central office administrators, more than even society would be willing to pay. I thought then, and still do today, that a complete restructuring of the profession was, and is in order: a change in the way schools are run, allowing for real teacher decision making power, true equality over important issues like the budget, with teachers having veto power over the principal. This would mean a significant change in the role of the principal, making teacher empowerment (and its byproduct, student learning) central to their jobs.

This really would mean a change in the status of teaching. So far, that cost *has* been more than anyone has been willing to pay. Teachers today still find their work lives shaped by the personality of whoever happens to be in the principal's office, someone they usually had no say in putting there. In Chicago various reform laws have altered the system-wide decision-making processes (which will be discussed later). Still, teachers are at the bottom of the ladder.

Where the bureaucracy meets the professional, where the (usually male) principal meets the (usually female) teacher, the latter are still at the mercy of the former. Whether the bureaucracy is centralized or decentralized, whether in Chicago or elsewhere around the country, the one reform that could revolutionize teaching and learning teacher empowerment—is not even on the agenda. It is hierarchical control, not professional control that prevails. The principals issue the system dictates and the teachers carry out them. These dictates—whether they are educationally sound or not, and the way they are imposed upon teachers—diminish teacher power.

My dissertation was finished. My questions continued. I wondered what kind of education system we could have if the teachers were officially empowered with the authority to be equal partners in the running of the school? What kinds of schools could we have if professionally powerful *teachers* ran them?

Chapter IV.
The AFT Years, 1983-91:
Lessons From Albert Shanker

I was cutting through my doctoral research at the University of Illinois at Chicago. I was also working part-time at the Chicago Teachers Union, coordinating the new CTU Graduate Program. Having the teachers' union provide classes on professional issues, was, I was about to find out, unique. One day, Jacqueline Vaughn, then the vice-president of the CTU, approached me about applying for a full time position at the American Federation of Teachers national office. It was a position, she told me, that they wouldn't offer me in all likelihood.

"They probably already have the person picked out," she said. "But Chicago is not well represented on our national staff, and I think you should apply for this position anyway."

It seemed a bit unusual—applying for something that apparently was out of my reach—but it would mean a trip to Washington, a city I had never seen, and an interview experience, and so what could be the harm?

I fell in love with Washington and ended up really, really wanting that job! The AFT interviewers made working there with them sound so interesting and so exciting. I came home hoping vainly that I would win out over the person with the inside track. I was absolutely heartbroken when I received their rejection letter.

One good thing came out of the episode, however. Marilyn Rauth and Eugenia Kemble had been interested in what I was doing with the CTU Graduate Program. They flew me into Washington several times to make presentations about it to union leaders and members at AFT's educational issues conferences. They also started having me make presentations on such topics as teacher stress and classroom management to AFT locals around the country whenever they needed a presenter.

A year later, Marilyn, now the Director of the AFT Educational Issues Department, called me saying that they had another full time position open. This one was a one-year appointment filling a vacancy of someone taking a leave of absence. She invited me to apply. The fact that it was only a one year position was actually a positive. I had loved Washington and was thrilled at the prospects of a new adventure. I wasn't sure I wanted to move permanently. The phone call came in June for a September startup. My new position was assistant director of the AFT Educational Issues Department. It was perfect timing, too. I had finished my dissertation research. Now all I had to do over the next three months was to finish writing the dissertation and defend it. The worst was over, right?

No. The worst was yet to come. I had yet to get the approval of Professor Bruce McPherson, one of the members of my dissertation committee. The way the process worked at UIC at that time was that you worked most closely with your dissertation chairperson. You only brought your work to the committee when it was reasonably complete. Most of the members of my committee thought the work was satisfactory. Except Professor McPherson. The other committee members said that they were ready to sign off on my work. Not Professor McPherson. Several times he returned chapters I had given him, stating that they were unacceptable and that he wouldn't sign off.

"What is wrong with my work?" I would plaintively ask him. He told me that my work lacked "intellectual passion." Oh my God, I thought, what is intellectual passion, and, even more important, how do I stick it into my bulky paper?

At last, after several unsuccessful exchanges of my paper, Professor McPherson told me that he had only one last suggestion before resigning from my committee. That meant going in one day and going over my paper. We would work chapter by chapter, word for word, for as long as it would take for me to "get it." At this point, feeling completely stupid, I said yes to him; to myself I said, "Anything to get out of here!"

The most excruciating, most torturous, most challenging, and ultimately most meaningful educational experience of my life was in the offing. It happened the Wednesday afternoon that I sat with Professor McPherson in an empty conference room in the UIC Education Building. There were no phones and no interruptions. We literally started at page one.

"What did you mean by this?" he would ask me when we arrived at a sentence or paragraph or idea which he found inadequate. I would explain, and he would bark, "Well, then, why didn't you say it like that?"

We moved slowly forward, and then there was the same question, "What did you mean by that?" and I would answer and he would yell, "Well, why in the world didn't you say it like that? There is too much of Smith and Jones and everybody else in here and not enough of you in here!"

Six grueling hours later we stopped, far short of going through the entire dissertation draft. Six hours! It was messy, it was painful, it was embarrassing. But it was the most memorable and the most meaningful educational experience of my life. Intellectual passion was me, I finally realized. It involved putting my ideas, my thoughts and my conclusions down, not simply spouting the conclusions of the intricacies of some expert or some theory. Yes, there was a place for the experts and the theories, but not to the exclusion of my own thinking. Intellectual passion was as simple, and as difficult, as that.

No teacher had ever taken time to challenge and help me that way. No teacher had invested so much interest and effort. Although I felt stupid, I also felt that he must have seen something in me to have tried so hard to find it. Those lessons have remained with me to this day. Another marker on the journey. Eventually, Professor McPherson approved all my chapters, one by one.

Now as much as I had tried to have everything done as I swept out of Chicago bound for the AFT and Washington, it didn't work out that way. Finding and sharing my intellectual passion took a little longer than I planned, and I ended up going to my new job in September. I returned to Chicago in January for the big dissertation defense. That normally dreaded experience was easy compared to my day with Professor McPherson. I'll never forget what he did for me.

Shortly before I left, tragedy struck me and my family. My younger brother, Jimmy, died in a car crash. I was the eldest of eight children and we were always a closely knit family. This loss devastated us. Jim was 26, a beautiful person with a bright future before him. Because he died instantly, none of us had a chance to say good-bye. We decided to each write a letter to him and kept those letters with him when we buried him. One thing I remember about all of our good-bye letters. Each of us wrote not only about how much he meant to us, but how he was always there for us, how we could always count on him. Now we had to try to go on without him. None of us will ever get over his loss. To this day when I see men around his age at children's soccer games or baseball games, I imagine Jim there. I imagine how much he would have enjoyed having a family and watching it grow. I imagine what a great dad he would have been.

As it happened, I arrived in Washington in September of 1983, shortly after the release of the highly acclaimed *A Nation at Risk* report. This groundbreaking report was done by President Reagan's Education Secretary Terrell Bell and his National Commission on Excellence in Education. This influential report on the state of education in this country decried the "rising tide of mediocrity" in our schools. It asserted that if another country did to us what we were doing to ourselves in education, we would consider it a unilateral act of war. The report found that many high school students did not possess the "higher order" intellectual skills that we should expect of them. Nearly 40 percent could not draw simple inferences; only one-fifth could write a persuasive essay; only one-third could solve a mathematical problem requiring several steps.

In 1984 another highly acclaimed study, High School, by Ernest Boyer argued that our high schools lacked a clear vision and vital mission. As a result, our students lacked the capacity to think critically and communicate effectively: "How can the relatively passive, docile roles of students prepare them to participate as informed, active and questioning citizens? How can we produce critical and creative thinking throughout a student's life when we so systematically discourage individuality in the classroom?" And in 1985 the Council on Economic Development issued a report *Investing in Our Children*. It asserted that "Mastery of the old basics…is not sufficient…and schools must make a greater effort to develop higher level skills such as problem solving, reasoning and learning ability."

These reports and studies confirmed my personal experience. It wasn't just me who had slipped by from grade to grade, degree to degree by playing the game. For years I simply figured out what teachers wanted to hear, or what I thought they wanted to hear. My process was to memorize for Friday's test and forget it all on Saturday Oh, you're supposed to have ideas of your own? Why hadn't I received that message sooner, long before I was a doctoral student: So it wasn't just me, but a broader indictment of the way we were doing education in this country.

Much to everyone's surprise, AFT President Albert Shanker, my new boss, did not come out swinging and railing against these indictments of our industry. He shocked everyone, especially AFT members, by agreeing with much in the reports. He actually saw the new attention to education, the push to rebuild public education instead of private options, and the inclination to put resources into this rebuilding, as very positive.

"I like the phrase 'a nation at risk'," he told his AFT colleagues at the 1983 convention in Los Angeles. "Those words put education on the same par as national defense. A nation at risk means that a country can go down. It can fall apart. We can lose it. It can disappear. Those are strong words. Those are good words. This is a period of great danger, and it is a period of unprecedented opportunity. To realize that opportunity, two things must happen: you need a program that focuses on quality. You can't just keep doing that same things that have proven unsuccessful. Second, we must be sure that the public doesn't see the teacher unions and collective bargaining as the obstacle to the improvement of education."

Shanker warned that the union must show a willingness to move far in the direction of these reports, (yes, even if it meant talking about forbidden issues like merit pay). Government and industry leaders, after investing time, effort and prestige on a program to rebuild American education should see results. Otherwise, Shanker believed, public education would lose its support and that there would be a massive move to try something else. Otherwise, "it would be all over." He meant the great experiment of public education in America.

His conclusion that day still inspires me. "Those organizations and individuals who are willing and able to participate, to compromise, and to talk will not be swept away. On the contrary, they will shape the direction of all the reforms and changes that are about to be made. That is what we in the AFT intend to do. We intend to be on board shaping the direction of every change in education. For the stakes are not just education. The stakes are certainly not just union. The stakes are the future of the country, and I know this union will rise to the challenge."

Such exciting ideas. Welcoming reform. Not wanting teachers and their unions to be seen as obstacles. In fact, positioning teachers and their unions to be part of the solution. Being "on board shaping the direction of every change in education." We teachers and our unions had the knowledge, the expertise, and even the *obligation* to be part of the solution. That was what Al Shanker believed and stood for.

I was in the right place at the right time. I was where I belonged. I was working for my union and, to use an old labor phrase, "the union makes us strong."

While Al Shanker was the head of the AFT, my immediate supervisor was Marilyn Rauth. I became the third of three assistant directors to Marilyn in the AFT's Educational Issues Department. There were only four professionals and three secretaries in that department then (and nearly forty staff members in that department today). That suggests the status of "education issues" in the AFT in 1983. Not yet a priority, but our time was coming. The two other assistant directors were Lovely Billups and Carolyn Trice. We all had been teachers and union members in various AFT locals. Marilyn was from Ohio and had taught somewhere in New Jersey. Carolyn had lived and taught in Missouri. Lovely had lived and taught in New York state. Then there was me, from Chicago. Our three secretaries included Theresa Soeth, Muriel Paulsen and Karla Smith. We were all simpatico, and everyone was generous to me, the new kid on the block.

The Ed Issues Department provided help to AFT locals on current issues, and a resource to other AFT national departments. For example, we wrote publications on current topics. We did presentations around the country at local union education conferences. We analyzed educational legislation and polices for local and state federations, and worked with other AFT departments on various campaigns where education issues were central. Lovely and the woman I was replacing had just completed an innovative, unique and important project for which the AFT had received federal funding. They called it ER&D (Educational Research and Dissemination).

ER&D had as its goal the important task of putting state-of-the-art research into the hands of practitioners. Historically this link has been weak. While we learn a lot of theory in teacher education programs, we teachers usually don't have access to current research findings unless we're in grad school. We therefore don't tend to think of ourselves as users of research. Researchers get rewarded for conducting sometimes esoteric research, not necessarily making sure it gets into the hands of the practitioners. The AFT wanted to do something about this disconnect, and secured a federal grant. AFT staff and some renowned researchers began an ambitious effort to not only to get the research into the hands of teachers. First they had to translate the research into user-friendly findings.

The research topics had to be identified. Then the writing "translating" began. This was followed by the design of training programs to share and discuss the research findings, followed by identifying whom to train, when and how. Because of the size of AFT—thousands of locals and hundreds of thousands of members—a training-of-trainers model was chosen as the most efficient approach.

But who to train? Union presidents, even if they were full time, were too busy to train members on educational research. They usually didn't have the time or that particular expertise. Few of the locals had even a part time person responsible for educational issues. Locals like New York City, Washington, D.C., and New Orleans had teachers who had been involved in the federally funded teacher center movement of the 1970's, and so those cities were selected for ER&D field testing. Finally, the AFT staff would train selected local union members, who in turn would set up a training program and train interested union members in their home locals.

Upon my arrival in Washington, I became part of the very first ER&D trainer-of-trainers program. They trained eleven of us. Eventually, I became a national trainer. The 10 other AFT members were teachers from locals in places like Corpus Christi, Texas, and Upstate New York.

I loved this strategy. From my own experience with the CTU Graduate program, I knew that AFT/CTU members were hungry for relevant, useful professional development experiences. The fact that they were being offered by the AFT only added credibility to the effort, in my opinion. The potential for something like ER&D seemed enormous to me. Given the extreme lack of high quality professional development I had observed as a professional development specialist, programs like this were urgently needed.

I also learned a great deal in that initial period from developing a publication summarizing all the various reforms that were being started because of all these national reform reports. The AFT was sponsoring a series of regional conferences for its leaders around the country. My publication was for background at these conferences. I began a lengthy telephone conversation with the directors of information from every state in the nation and obtained a detailed overview of state-level reform activity. The regional reform conferences were very stimulating and exciting. I was able to attend all of them, each with its unique cast of regional characters, governors, business leaders and local union leaders. The state of education and its necessary reforms were on the union's agenda. While putting the State Reforms publication together and participating in these conferences, I kept thinking about the parallels between my painful experience with Professor McPherson and the messages of these reports. Too many of our students were graduating from high school without the necessary higher level thinking skills, the critical thinking skills needed for their future, they said.

I went to Marilyn to make my case for writing a small AFT brochure on critical thinking and how teachers could incorporate it into their teaching. I thought that this could be my little contribution to expanding intellectual passion in the world. Marilyn gave me the go ahead, and I began with relish. When my "small brochure" moved beyond 100 pages, I realized that perhaps something longer was evolving. Before long we had a book, a training-of-trainers program, a quarterly network newsletter, and a cadre of 200 trained teachers. Thanks to Marilyn's talent for letting her staff run with ideas, and to Lovely's ER&D training-of-trainers model, the AFT Critical Thinking Project began.

This project was an experience for me. My brochure became a regular AFT paperback book, co-written by Professor Richard Paul of Sonoma State University, a nationally known critical thinking advocate, and myself. Then, in true ER&D fashion, I worked with AFT teacher members to create a 45-hour professional development course for teachers. We offered this training in many AFT locals for university graduate credit. All of my experience as a teacher and as a professional development specialist was put to the test in designing the content of the training program. I was grateful for guidance and direction from an outstanding group of Washington, D.C. teachers who had volunteered to work on the project with me. We were a team on a mission. Individually, any of us could have written a 45-hour training program. It would have paled in comparison to the one we thrashed out together. We fought and argued over how to present ideas, which examples to use, what questions to ask. We were almost brilliant, or so we thought.

The next step was field testing. One of the first groups of teacher trainers that I presented the program to was particularly—and painfully—critical. Seasoned teacher-trainers from all around New York state, they were used to a substantially different format from the one I was presenting. At certain times during the week long training with them, I wondered if the program, or I, would survive it. Yet my gut feeling was that these seasoned veterans had something to teach me to make the program better.

I received specific, pointedly critical feedback (e.g., not enough detailed instruction for the trainers to do the training activities, suggestions for improving the activities). Determined, I returned to Washington to rewrite the first edition of the training, based on their responses. We were scheduled to get back together the following November on a weekend during which I presented the changes to them and held my breath, waiting for their responses. They approved and agreed that, with the changes they had recommended, the program was improved. It was even good!

After that, AFT teachers from all over the U.S. went through the AFT Critical Thinking Project training. Members reported that they found it useful, valuable in their work with students. Over several summers, teachers from perhaps 100 locals were trained. They took the manual and materials back home to their unions and offered courses for teachers to enhancing the critical thinking skills of their students. The quarterly newsletter highlighted current articles of critical thinking and shared lesson plans showing how various teachers were incorporating more critical thinking for their students in various subject areas. In several districts, they brought in the AFT at the expense of the school district to teach the Critical Thinking Course as an ongoing professional development program. Administrators were turning to the AFT for something positive. We were gaining ground.

As coordinator of the project, I was able to work with hundreds of dedicated teacher union members, and even school administrators. They believed, as I did, that the union had to take the lead on educational and professional issues. As Al Shanker had said, we needed to be seen as part of the solution, not part of the problem.

Other highlights of my work at the AFT included a media campaign in the state of Alabama against a legislative proposal advocating merit pay. This included airplane hops to press conferences in four or five cities around the state, all on the same day, with the leadership of the AFT in Alabama. I was the State federation's "national expert" at these press conferences on why merit pay has never worked in the past and was not a good idea now. (Inwardly, I chuckled at the "expert" designation, remembering a joke we used to tell when I was a professional development specialist in districts around Chicago. An expert was anyone who lived more than forty miles away.)

During this campaign, we also stopped in Birmingham to hold a press conference and to lobby state legislators against the bill. I had never experienced anything like that day. Zoom in, be part of a team talking to very interested reporters, zoom out and go to another city to do it all again. The AFT was very small in Alabama since Alabama is a "right to work," anti-union state and dominated by the National Education Association(NEA). Yet that day at least, we were a powerful force.

I also made presentations to AFT locals overseas. I had been surprised to learn that AFT represents union members teaching in

Department of Defense schools. I was able to go to Belgium, England, Italy and Panama to teach AFT courses and provide assistance to AFT locals in those countries. Meeting and talking to teachers who had been living and teaching overseas for decades was an experience in itself. They had led very rich and interesting lives and were exceptionally grateful to have their national union provide resources and support to them.

A disturbing trip to Panama stands out in my mind. Noriega was in power. At the time of my visit, there was a travel advisory. Still, the local president had urged me to come ahead. He had gone to considerable trouble to get his members Department of Defense Education credits for taking the weekend course we were offering. For a little extra protection, he had me stay in military barracks on a Department of Defense installation, and he personally drove me around anywhere that I needed to go. The extra security was a little eerie.

During that weekend training, I used Martin Luther King's "I Have a Dream" speech in a Socratic seminar, something I often did in the Critical Thinking training. We listened to a tape of the speech and then started discussing some of its powerful ideas. People seemed a little reluctant to talk about the speech. Someone said something about what was done to Martin Luther King, and the next thing I knew accusations I hadn't heard in thirty years started being hurled around the room. The discussion became more than heated.

Things calmed down after some discussion and some further explanation of the seminar process. It was unsettling, however, that something I had considered a cherished and non-controversial piece could have elicited such vehement reactions. That night, over dinner with the local officers, the president told me that many people there still carried the same feelings and attitudes they brought with them 30 years ago. This wasn't about race in Panama, since the Americans in Panama kept pretty much to themselves, but about race in the U.S. decades ago. For many of them, not much had changed. It was a lesson in culture clash for me.

Other AFT assignments included working hand in hand with staff from the AFT's Organizing Department on many union activities, organizing campaigns and current issues. I really enjoyed getting an up close look at campaigns to organize new members (or steal them from the NEA), at membership drives, negotiation preparations, and leadership training.

The Organizing Department had about forty "national representatives" or "nat reps" who lived all around the U.S. These nat reps were assigned to work in various places for various periods, sometimes a few months and sometimes longer. They would fly into their assignments from home Monday and return home Friday, a different kind of commuting. These staff members were leader-types from AFT locals who had joined the national staff. They worked primarily in places that were not large enough to have their own full-time staff for such things as negotiating and campaigning. They were the best at what they did.

One assignment I really enjoyed was working with AFT National representative Don Kuehn in Chelsea, Massachusetts during the big Boston University (BU) takeover of the Chelsea Public Schools system. Don coordinated the Chelsea Federation of Teachers(CFT) response to the takeover and handled their negotiations with BU. I came in several times to help Don position the CFT there to be a cooperative part of the new governance process. We did this by providing leadership training for the CFT's officers and executive board members. We also negotiated for and jointly offered professional development courses with BU to strengthen teachers' instructional skills. Don had such a confident and almost Clint Eastwood style of working that it was fun to watch these university types deal with him. Thanks to Don, even BU saw an advantage in working collaboratively with the union on some things.

The Educational Issues Department also worked on paraprofessional issues. For example, Tom Moran, a colleague in the AFT Organizing Department, and I worked together on a paraprofessional project. We successfully co-wrote a grant to the federal government for a labor-management cooperation grant. It enabled paraprofessionals from the Albuquerque Teacher Assistants Federation to create a career ladder program for their members. Even the feds were recognizing the value and potential of cooperative efforts between labor and management and were providing incentives for making it happen.

A career ladder is a series of steps paraprofessionals can take to gain greater roles and responsibilities in their positions in exchange for higher salary. Sometimes it is a route for paraprofessionals to become teachers. Tom and I used to visit Albuquerque once a month, for a year or so, after we won the grant. Our role then was to help the work of the joint labor-management committee. The purpose of the committee was to develop the elements of the career ladder program that the Albuquerque Teachers Assistants had wanted and waited for so long. We had to facilitate the work of people who usually sat on opposite sides of the table with adversarial agendas, but who now had a common agenda. This was often quite challenging. Yet I think we all realized that somehow we were on the verge of something new and important in labor relations.

While I worked there, the AFT's governance structure was made up of the President and Secretary-Treasurer, a five-member Executive Committee, and a 38-member Executive Council. Today it also includes a third national officer, a 40-member Executive Council and Policy Councils (representing the various AFT constituency groups: teachers paraprofessionals, higher education professors, nurses, etc.) The Executive Council is made up of various local presidents from around the country. It meets four times a year. Those meetings were highlights for me.

As president, Al Shanker, ran those meetings. They allowed staff members to attend (observe, really) when they were held in Washington, on the theory that we needed to know the policy and direction of the organization. Meeting participants included union presidents from all parts of the country, people who were used to running things, getting their way and being top dogs. The Council meetings were provocative, often argumentative, sometimes funny, and never boring.

While the Council got its work done, Shanker also used these meetings as teaching experiences. He invited guest speakers from all kinds of places, representing all kinds of fields, on policy topics he felt the Council needed to be informed about. He brought in nationally known doctors and researchers who gave members their read on the future of health care in this country, for example. He brought in experts to give their take on the technologies of the future and their implications for education. He brought in researchers who had done comparative studies on U.S. and Japanese education. He brought in union leaders from Eastern European countries before the 1989 fall of Russian Communism to share their experiences and discuss their needs. Going to these meetings was like getting another college education.

Shanker's agenda seemed to be opening people's minds to the future, to ideas, to theories, to best and worst case scenarios to help them make informed decisions about the organization nationally and locally. Often the speakers would provide information to help him sell a particular plan or policy. Usually, there was debate and argument over which way to go, particularly when it came to matters of education reform. Not all the Council members saw education reform as opportunity, as he did. Few were as forward looking and visionary as Al Shanker.

One example is classic. In the early 1980's, Shanker had invited the president of the Toledo Federation of Teachers (TFT), someone not on the Executive Council, to a Council meeting. He was asked to present a new initiative of the TFT called the Toledo Intern Intervention Program. This program was the result of a ten-year struggle beteween the TFT leadership and their school district administration. TFT leaders wanted to establish a joint labor-management program of support and assistance to new teachers and to teachers experiencing difficulties in the classroom.

I knew that new teachers were badly in need of guidance and support as they embark on one of the most challenging of professions. I also knew of the total lack of resources for teachers who were struggling in the classroom. Principals were usually no help in mentoring new teachers or shoring up the skills of teachers in trouble. They just eased out, or forced out, those that they didn't want in their schools. These poor souls would go from school to school until their weaknesses became painfully apparent and the next principal, instead of helping them, would advise them to find another school. The practice was so rampant it even had its own catch phrase—"the dance of the lemons."

Well, the TFT had negotiated a program that would be an equal responsibility of the union and the administration. Under the program, all new Toledo teachers would have a master teacher assigned to them to provide guidance and support and role modeling for their first two years of teaching. Then a recommendation would be made to the joint labor-management committee whether or not they should receive tenure. Teachers in trouble, as identified by their principals and union representatives, would get a mentor assigned to them to help them strengthen their skills for one year. At the end of the year, if the person had improved, great. If not, a recommendation was made to the committee whether to give the person more time or to counsel them out of the profession. Surprisingly, under the new program, they refused more teachers tenure, or counseled out, than when the administration had sole responsibility for new and troubled teachers.

They almost threw out Dal Lawrence, the TFT president, of the AFT Executive Council meeting. The union was involved in peer review? The union would be involved in teacher evaluation and even be responsible for teachers losing their jobs? No! These ideas were an anathema to most of the AFT leaders sitting around the council table. It was heresy to them to think that the union should play any kind of role when it came to evaluating teachers.

Dal Lawrence argued that the union had a bad reputation with the public for protecting incompetent teachers. He tried to tell his colleagues around the table that when the union was involved, union members had more help when they needed help. Teachers also did a better job than management when it came to helping teachers who might not otherwise make it. Wasn't this better than having to defend an incompetent teacher that management failed to identify as incompetent before it was too late? Union members didn't like working with incompetent teachers any more than the parents wanted their children to be taught by one. If we were a union of professionals, wasn't it, or shouldn't it be, a responsibility of the union to police the profession? To prevent teacher incompetence rather than sometimes having to defend the indefensible?

Dal Lawrence didn't care if the members of the AFT Executive Council thought he was a traitor to the movement. He went straight ahead with his agenda. Years later he proudly told me that the Toledo Intern-Intervention Program was the single most important thing his members thought he accomplished. Not that it was without problems. Not that he didn't have to threaten to cancel the program when management was recalcitrant about other issues. **Because of that experience, today I don't think these kinds of peer review programs can work unless there is real equality between labor and management, at every level.** But in Toledo the program helped weed out people who his own members thought shouldn't be working with children. It boosted the union's public image of a union that cared about the quality of teacher professionalism and the quality of education.

Funny enough, even after the cold reception of the AFT Council to the idea, a peer review program sprang up in Cincinnati. Then another one sprung up in Rochester, New York, and elsewhere. It seemed that some of those sitting at that AFT Executive Council meeting that day were listening. As the reform movement of the 1980's heated up, the idea of peer assistance, peer evaluation and the union's role in evaluating teachers became an accepted, even expected, idea. Today many locals from which the most resistance emanated now have some form of involvement in teacher evaluation.

Nevertheless, that resistance became a theme throughout that period and created much division among the members of the AFT leadership across the country. "We are an organization of rough, tough, organizing, negotiating, bread-and-butter-only unionists. We have been through the wars and made hard-fought and hard won gains," was the message from one side. "We aren't about to jeopardize those gains with any of this touchy-feely 'professional issues' garbage."

"But if we aren't part of the solution, we will be tarred and feathered as part of the problem," the other side responded.

This division played itself out in many of the union's activities, policies and positions during that period. Yet Al Shanker continued to be at the forefront of the debate. He insisted that the "professionalization" of teaching and the union's role in leading it meant life or death for the future of public education. He received a standing ovation at the 1984 AFT convention for the following remarks:

"It may very well be that if we can consider a movement toward professionalizing teachers, we will be able to show other workers and other unions that it is possible to create a model where a union is looked upon not merely as an institution devoted to protecting jobs and self interest. We'll show that a union really has two faces: one is for protection and security and economic well being—and there is nothing wrong with those; they are part of the American way of life—but the other side represents standards and excellence and professionalism, which includes participation and self-governance...The job that we face in the future will be as difficult as the one we faced in the past. But as I see it, the professionalization of teaching in the next 10 or 20 years is life or death for the future of public education—just the way building the union 20 or 30 years ago probably gave us the ability to protect public schools over that period...I am sure that all of you who have taken unpopular union positions before, after debating and after rethinking these issues, will champion this, at present, unpopular cause and help us build education not only as a strong place for us as a union, but as a great and respected profession."

Shanker equated union building and profession building, an almost shocking connection at the time. He emphasized that the future of the union and even the public school system was at stake. Thanks to Albert Shanker, professionalizing teaching became one of the war cries of the 1980's, a goal that involved more than teacher salaries and peer review. The notions of participation and self governance as part of being a professional began to take root. In places as different as Dade County Florida and Hammond, Indiana, school-based management and shared decision making started finding their way into union contracts. In 1985, he called for the creation of a National Board of Professional Teaching Standards which has, in fact, become a reality. This Board has already made an impact on the status of the profession.

Shanker's commitment to a strong union and a strong profession never wavered. He knew that you could only go about the business of building the profession from a position of strength. Once he told a group of members, "We'd never be sitting at the table talking about professionalism if we hadn't built a strong union, if we didn't have collective bargaining, if we didn't have contracts, if we didn't have strong political action. We wouldn't count." Yet he realized that "it became evident that the bargaining process was severely limited in its ability to deal with some of the issues that were most important to teachers."

For me, his most moving speech was about a Martian. "A Martian who happened to be visiting Earth soon after the United States was founded would not have given this country much of a chance of surviving. He would have predicted that this new nation, whose inhabitants were of different races, who spoke different languages and who followed different religions, wouldn't remain one nation for long. They would end up fighting and killing each other. Then, what was left of each group would set up its own country, just as has happened many other times in many other places. But that didn't happen. Instead we became a wealthy and powerful nation—the freest the world has ever known. Millions of people have risked their lives to come here, and they continue to do so today.

"Public schools played a big role in holding our nation together. They brought children of different races, languages, religions and cultures and gave them a common language and a common purpose. We have not outgrown our need for this; far from it. Today Americans come from more different countries and speak more languages than ever before. Whenever the problems connected with school reform seem especially tough, I think about what public education gave me— a kid who couldn't even speak English when I entered first grade. I think about what it has given me and can give to countless numbers of other kids like me. And I know that keeping public education together is worth whatever effort it takes."

My years at the AFT were inspiring, stimulating, exciting. Working for the union became almost like a religion to me. We had a mission, a dogma, true believers all over the country who lived and breathed, and believed, in union. I loved and greatly respected the national staff members I worked with, and the AFT leaders and members I had the honor to meet and work with all over the country. We had a common belief system. We felt that we were part of an extremely important— even life and death—effort to expand the union and save the public school system.

I was also part of the union within the union, the AFT Staff Union (AFTSU). This was the union that negotiated our bread and butter issues with Al Shanker himself. I was a union steward for AFTSU and, in that capacity, I helped AFTSU members when they had work problems and grievances to be filed, which did happen. With members scattered all across the country, we were only able to meet twice a year, when we had national staff meetings. The AFT leadership built time into those meetings for our AFTSU meetings which were always interesting because of the widely varying experiences, assignments and perspectives of our membership.

I ended up staying with the AFT in Washington for eight years, and that experience profoundly influenced me. I went East as a bright-eyed, naive, intellectually open thirty-two year old. I returned to the Midwest as a confident, outspoken, intellectually stronger forty-year-old. When I first arrived at the AFT, I was impressed by the leaders and staff there who knew who they were and could argue their positions with conviction. I had gone through almost all of graduate school feeling like an imposter. I had felt that, eventually, someone would find me out as not deserving to be there, though I did. At the AFT I was thrust into many situations where I had to think on my feet. I had to present, debate and argue AFT positions on many issues with a variety of groups: merit pay, peer review, school-based management, teacher quality, and more. Over time, with these experiences, I became more sure of myself. Increasingly, I would be one of the more vocal people in the room. I would find myself with more background or more information or more ideas than the university professors, administrators, or others at meetings or conferences. Once, despite myself, I took an unpopular stand at one of our AFTSU meetings over whether or not to censure one of our colleagues. After the meeting, I expected some colleagues to disprove of me or maybe even shun me. To my surprise, they treated me with greater respect than ever before.

I had so many powerful role models. Marilyn and Lovely were strong, articulate and knowledgeable colleagues, and friends. Eugenia Kemble returned to the AFT after a hiatus at the AFL-CIO and took over as Director of the Educational Issues Department upon Marilyn's departure. She became boss, mentor and friend.

During my AFT tenure, I spent a bit of time in Illinois. I made many presentations for the Illinois Federation of Teachers and the Chicago Teachers Union, and some of the suburban and downstate AFT-IFT locals. I kept in quite regular touch with my old friend John Kotsakis at the CTU. By now, Jacqui Vaughn was president of the CTU, and John was the Assistant to the President for Educational Issues. He had advanced from the position of Field Representative, which he was when I first interviewed him, to Director of the Field Services and then to Assistant to the President. He used to joke whenever I called him that he didn't want to hear any more ideas from me about what he should do next. Every time I had heard about some exciting new program (the Toledo plan, school-based management, etc.), I called him and suggested that the CTU do it, too. One day a call from him turned out to be a request to help him secure a grant to create a professional development initiative within the CTU. The Illinois state legislature had passed a school reform law in 1988 that changed the governance structures of the Chicago Public Schools. This included some roles for teachers on newly forming Local School Councils and Professional Personnel Advisory Committees. Jacqui and John wanted the union to help prepare teachers for these new roles in the schools.

Eugenia okayed my request to make six monthly visits to Chicago to facilitate the work of a CTU committee charged with imagining what the initiative would be. The committee had a majority of CTU members on it. John also realized that it would benefit from having the participation from various local universities, reform groups, and the state and local boards of education. We began each meeting with a guest speaker to inform ourselves about the models and the possibilities. We would then deliberate. Over time, the idea of a union teacher academy emerged, a center that would have as its mission the stimulation and support of teacher leadership in education reform. John and I then went to work on writing a grant to the MacArthur Foundation for the teacher academy.

One and a half years later, John was at a conference and ran into the new MacArthur Foundation education officer who asked to get together with John sometime. John told him not unless it was to talk about the grant proposal we had submitted eighteen months ago. Peter Martinez agreed. The next thing I knew, John was calling me to say that the Foundation had approved the grant. He asked me to come home and help him start it. Leaving the AFT was truly painful. I cried all the way through my going away party. But it was time to go home. John and I had work to do.

Chapter V.
Sojourn to Poland, 1990:
Lessons From Teacher Solidarity

July 15, 1990

We sit at the gate at Washington's Dulles airport. Our plane is about to pull away, headed for Frankfurt. Then it's on to Warsaw, Poland for me. I wonder, what am I doing here? Am I crazy to be going to Poland, alone, for two weeks? By the time I'm back here, I'll know the answer to those questions. I think it will be a positive experience, though this morning I awoke with butterflies. Like almost everyone else, I've been so moved by the stunning events in Eastern Europe. I've also been inspired by the Polish and Czechoslovakian visitors speaking to AFT groups here. I am proud to be part of an organization that believes in freedom, believes in these people. The AFT has helped them through the hard times, and now through the victorious times. I also believe that we must stay involved, long after the thrill of the "velvet revolutions" subsides. It will take a long, grinding time for these countries to rebuild. But this trip is not just for the "political me." It's also for the "private me."

July 19, 1990

Here is it, four days later, and I'm finally sitting down to write again. I guess that says something about how busy and enjoyable these days have been. When I arrived in Warsaw on Monday afternoon, I hopped into a cab for my hotel with enough confidence to bargain with the cabdriver for the fare (as they had advised me to do). I could strike out, unconcerned, in a strange country where I did not even know the language. I've really enjoyed the people on the tour, most from Canada, Australia, England, and the States. For complete strangers, we really have fun, on the bus, over meals, and over drinks at the end of a long, satisfying day. I am relishing my own company, too. Thus, I'm skipping part of the tour to do my own thing. In a few minutes I have a meeting at the Solidarity offices here in Krakow.

July 23, 1990

Tuesday morning we had lunch in what they advertised as a country inn. It was a strange place, in a most unusual structure at the end of a block of hideous Communist-built housing projects. Despite appearances, I'm glad to confess, we had the best potato pancakes I have ever eaten. Wednesday found us in Krakow, and I skipped the bus tour to wander around and explore the town on my own. Thursday we went through the Krakow castle, cathedral and market square, and then out to Nova Huta, the Communist' "model suburb." This was the most memorable and disturbing part of the day. Bleak, dehumanizing, hopeless, resigned, are a few of the words that come to mind. This depressing suburb was one relentless "Cabrini Green" housing project after another. The pollution from the surrounding factories-for which Nova Huta was built-has already corroded statues and buildings in nearby Krakow. The pollution level here is 11,000 times the standard for Western Europe! What must it be doing to the lungs of children?

July 24, 1990

Friday was our most important day. We traveled to Auschwitz and Bierkenau. Along the way our bus broke down, and we lost an hour and a half of valuable time. Our tour guide, Barbara, admitted that she is an extremely nervous person, with many "complexes." While they were repairing the bus, she explained a little bit about herself and had us in tears. When she was 12 years old, she was part of a group of people on the streets of Warsaw whom the Nazis indiscriminately herded together *and lined up. The Nazis periodically took actions like this to terrorize the population and keep them in a constant state of anxiety and submission. Because she was small, Barbara was last in line. One of the German shoulders came up to her and motioned for her to run away. With incredible danger to himself, he set a 12-year-old girl free. She went on to survive the terrible war, with its occupation by the Nazis, and the uninvited imposition of Communism. Hearing part of her life story, we could begin to understand why this woman in her mid sixties fell apart when something unexpected happened. That one delay produced a domino effect of delays, with their associated problems and headaches. She never quite recovered her poise and confidence.*

Words are totally inadequate to describe Auschwitz: the standing rooms where up to 60 people were stuffed overnight to be suffocated or stampeded to death; the insidious 4-man cells for standing in pitch-black closeness for punishment; the eerie mountains of shoes, abandoned eyeglasses and hairbrushes. Man's inhumanity to man. Now I know more about the true meaning of that phrase.

July 25, 1990

We visited a salt mine, hundreds of feet below the earth, filled with carvings that seemed real crystal, but were only salt. Chamber after chamber revealed statues and figures of heroes and royalty, but the climax was the final chamber where we all heaved a collective gasp of astonishment. We were standing in a complete underground cathedral, replete with gorgeous chandeliers and statues and marble-looking floors, all made from salt. This will be considered one of the wonders of the world when the world discovers it.

*Our trip included Zakopane, and Czestochowa, with its Black Madonna. Czestochowa is known as the spiritual center of Poland. We visited Chopin's home, and then went back to Warsaw. We all went over to the Marriott for a familiar American-style meal complete with friendly waiters, bread **and** butter, coffee **and** cream. Tomorrow is the last day of our bus tour and time for good-byes, and on to the second half of my trip—on my own, connecting with teacher Solidarity contacts.*

July 28, 1990

I skipped the morning tour of the Warsaw Palace, and instead I went to Rosalin, a suburb of Warsaw, with Eric, a fellow AFT staff member. We wanted to observe the morning training session being sponsored by the Education for Democracy Foundation. I was thrilled as I watched the Poles—whom AFT staff members had trained—now training other Solidarity members in the fundamentals of running an aboveground union. Through the translations I learned a lot about how the Polish school system was structured and problems they were confronting in this new era. Some of the problems were totally foreign to us (i.e., Communist party principals). Some were surprisingly similar (i.e., teachers wanting more decision-making power). This informative day was topped off by our tour group's farewell dinner at the Europeiski Hotel and our good-byes. It had been a stunning tour and a great way to get an overview and a sense of Poland. I am glad I took the tour, and now I am ready for the next part of this adventure, whatever that will be...

July 29, 1990

My colleague, Eric, responding to my request to meet Teacher Solidarity leaders and learn about educational and union issues in Poland, had made arrangements and contacts for me. I spent the morning reading a little and shopping for souvenirs. I didn't know whether I would end up back in Rosalin or Wroclaw for the night. It turned out to be Wroclaw. After getting my train ticket and having a quick lunch with Marec and Margaret, I found myself in seat #55 on my way to a strange city. Gryzina, someone I had met for 10 minutes at Rosalin and who didn't speak any English, was supposed to meet me. I also didn't have a clue what I would be doing in Wroclaw, but Eric had told me to trust these people, so I did. The unknown beckoned with both hands.

July 30, 1990

The five-hour journey to Wroclaw enabled me to put a big dent in Michener. What a thrill to read his book about Poland in Poland. It has created a rich context for my observations and experiences. Arriving in

Wroclaw I found no one who seemed to be looking for me. After an hour of conspicuous waiting, I considered going to a nearby hotel, but how would I tell Gryzina (who doesn't speak English) where I was on the telephone? I decided to take a chance that someone at her number might speak English, and I called the number they had given me. Thankfully, someone did, and Gryzina's friend, Anna, came and picked me up. She brought me to what would be home for the next few days. It was a former Communist training center out just a small distance from the old part of town. The center was now a new teacher' college where I had a comfortable dorm room.

Today Anna, who speaks English reasonably well, came for me. She brought me to her home where we had a breakfast of French coffee, ham, pate, bread, and her homemade jam. Scrumptious. Then we went off on a tour of this beautiful, untouched-by-the-war city. Anna was busy in the afternoon, so I was on my own. I wandered and explored and shopped for amber, the sparkling, golden stone found in Poland. When I became hungry, I stopped at a restaurant, only to find the menu (surprise, surprise!) entirely in Polish. I made some guesses and ended up with some delicious trout and potatoes. I managed to find my way "home" on the tram. I only needed to show my address a few times to people when I came to a crossroads and didn't know which way to turn. That night I finished **Poland.**

July 31, 1990

Today my "driver" picked me up at 10:00 a.m. I had a brief meeting with Gryzina, and then we were off to another meeting with teachers from the Wroclaw region of Solidarity. Joanna's apartment was in one of the old housing projects. These projects were smaller, bleaker versions of the newer, bigger, uglier ones dotting the country. The entrances were as dingy, gray, and forbidding as I imagine those of prisons to be. However, when you are inside, when once you step over the threshold, you enter a warm Polish home, rich in color and memories that the Communists could not diminish. Looking out the window at the desolate landscape of building after building, I think that this must be the view from the worst housing projects back home in Chicago. Yet the people in these apartments are teachers and university professors and union activists, not welfare recipients. This was a statement of the fear and contempt in which the Communists held the intelligentsia. The oppressors tried to keep those with fine minds and educations impoverished and impotent. We began an hours-long discussion of Polish and American education and unionism. It would be the highlight of my trip.

Imagine that you're back in school again, but this time the school is designed to impede, not enhance, learning. What does this school look like?

Well, first, there is lots of regimentation; students walk in straight lines and sit passively in silence in perfectly straight rows of desks and chairs. There is lots of standardization; everyone is taught the same thing at the same time in the same way. There are lots of facts and figures—the ones considered important by the establishment—to be memorized and then forgotten. The classrooms are sparsely furnished, with little or nothing in the way of equipment or modern technology. Teachers *and* students are told what to do, when to do it, and how to do it. Virtually every decision throughout your entire years of schooling is made for you. The structure, the routine, the rigid rules and regulations, and the endless memorization prevent you from ever having to think seriously for yourself.

The teachers in this school are selected based on their own success in this system. They go along with being told what to do, when to do it, and how to do it. They are poorly paid, and their working conditions are marginal. This ensures that only those who can't find jobs elsewhere (or the totally committed zealots) take the job. This also ensures that most of the gifted and talented candidates, those most like to question the system, would not even bother applying. Nobody, including the principal—the principal selected by headquarters—has to think for himself or herself in this system.

No, I'm not talking about an urban school system in the United States at low ebb. This is a real-life description of what the Polish schools were like under Communism. The Communists did this to the Poles. To the extent that there are parallels-if different in degree and kind-what is our excuse in the United States?

As Poland continues its incredible, difficult transition from dictatorship to democracy, its most important task is teaching the next generation about democracy. This is a daunting challenge. Why? When Communism fell, no one less than 50 had ever experienced democracy. The Communists had seen the schools as the most effective means of inculcating Polish children with Communist views; that's why they controlled everything that happened in them. For example, they forced the children to take eight years of Russian language. They taught their own revised version of history and stuffed children's heads with ideology and propaganda. They forced them to attend party festivities and festivals and to join Communist youth groups. Yet, though they saw the schools as valuable tools for the party, they underfunded them. "The reason for this is easy to understand," said Anna, ruefully. "It's much easier to rule in a country where the people are stupid."

If you emphasize mindless conformity and rote learning infused with ideological lies, you can keep the people suppressed, compliant, and complacent. Right? Well, perhaps for a while. But as we all know now, after the astonishing events of 1989, the answer to that question is for a while, but not the whole answer. (You can't fool all of the people all of the time. True, Mr. Lincoln.)

The Communists had underestimated the tradition of underground resistance in Poland and the Pole's fierce and historic love of freedom. Life was intentionally constructed to be so difficult that the basic day-to-day struggle for survival became the most important thing. Despite this, the people fought back and eventually, they won.

That love of freedom and resistance to oppression dates back to the relentless efforts of other countries, over the centuries, to try to subjugate Poland. Often, the Poles didn't even have Polish kings. They would bring in kings "from the outside" so that no one Pole would have too much power over the others. They also had the famous "liberum veto," or rule by unanimity, which meant that just one vote in their parliament could negate the entire work of the body. While this is an impossible way to govern, it exemplifies their tremendous resistance to having something imposed on them.

Of course, it was the upper, not the lower classes, who loved this freedom for themselves. Freedom was not for peasants. Yet around the time of the American Revolution, Poland was moving in a similar direction, with a constitution with rights for gentry and peasants alike. It has been said that this irrepressible love of freedom was Poland's downfall-contributing to its 1793 partition, for example. Until its current, still very fragile efforts, Poles have had difficulty reconciling this love of freedom with the responsibility of governing themselves.

With only two short decades of turbulent independence between the two World Wars, Poland was again taken over, this time by the Nazi reign of terror. One quarter of the population was murdered in World War II, including many of the six million Jews ultimately annihilated by Hitler's orders in Poland and Germany. City after city was destroyed. Still, despite the terror and destruction, the Polish underground developed, grew, and thrived. It has been said that under the Nazi occupation, sabotage in Poland became an art form. James Michener has described the Poles as the world's master saboteurs. He said they learned to devise the most clever ways to circumvent the rule of the Nazi, and then the Communist oppressor. They included laziness on the job, breaking their machines, irritating their bosses. The Nazis eliminated the Jews, the intelligentsia, the leaders. The Russians eliminated anyone they thought might be a threat to their totalitarian regime. Yet families secretly passed on the truth to their children. Brave teachers taught real history to their students. The underground resistance-in the form of Solidarity-emerged, and thrived, and won.

Here were my contemporaries. They had risked their lives, and the lives of their families and friends, to be free. Here were brave teachers who had gone to jail for their beliefs, who persisted in their illegal underground activity-distributing newspapers, building their union, teaching their truth-despite the dangers to themselves. I was humbled in their presence.

"Where did you find the courage?" I asked them.

"The struggle didn't just start with us," Joanna, a Teacher Solidarity activist, told me over the meal her mother had prepared for us. "The Polish people fought this oppression ever since the war, when rebuilding was the most important thing. And in the homes, the parents taught their children. But it was very confusing for me, too," she said wistfully. "My parents taught me one thing, and the school a completely different thing. I began to think that the school must be right. It wasn't until I spent some time in Canada, and read some books that they banned here, that I began to realize what was going on."

"It was very difficult," said Isabella, her colleague, a history teacher known for her efforts to teach real history to her students. "They constructed our lives to keep us from having time to think. For example, assigning jobs across the city so the maximum time would be spent getting there and back every day. Things were so difficult here that day-to-day struggles became the most important thing."

"And how did you find the courage to ignore the history that you were supposed to teach?" I asked, knowing that they watched teachers who deviated from the program, harassed, threatened.

"I just hated the Communists," she replied. "My father had been a member but they had kicked him out because he was too honest. I guess it's just my nature to resist that sort of authoritarianism. I have taught nothing but the real history," she continued, proudly. "I had a very liberal director [principal], who looked the other way and did not interfere with me. I relied, not on the official textbooks, of course, but on books obtained from the underground. Of course, during the first year of martial law, the authorities observed me on nine different occasions.

"During martial law, I **requested** to be evaluated," said Joanna. "I needed evidence that I was a good teacher in case they tried to do anything to me for my political beliefs and activities."

"Under martial law I never had such a good time," laughed Anna, the university administrator. "So many meetings and parties, all at night because we couldn't be on the street past 8:00 p.m. You see," she continued, emphasizing with her hands, "they push us down and we try to jump back up again." She frowned, lost in thought for a moment. "The really bad time," she said, when she finally continued, "was between 1983 and 1987, when people relaxed. The police then increased their pressure, constantly coming around to see if we were hiding people from the underground in our homes. I had a very bad time with the police then." Her voice trailed off with the memory.

At the time of my visit in 1990, teachers were still afraid. In the cities, 50 percent of the teachers in any given school were Solidarity members or supporters. Nationally, however, only about 18% of the teachers belonged to the union. Because most of the school directors were communist Party members, they tended to hire other party members, or those they felt that they could control. Standards for entry into the profession eroded; they were reduced to political considerations, for the most part. Solidarity membership was lowest out in the rural areas, where the teachers still were afraid to challenge the directors who had hired them. In those schools, teacher members of the official Communist union—many unqualified but owing their jobs to the party—supported their directors.

Even those who had fought so valiantly for the chance to be free didn't know any other system. They recognized that they themselves were products of the old system. "Every day you touch something from the past," said Anna, thoughtfully. "Though we fought it, it's still in us."

Poland's real hope, and its future, lies with its children. How does a country approach the challenge of teaching the next generation in such a state of transition? The problems are many, including a public mistrust of the state schools that bear the taint of ideology and propaganda; the decimation of the teaching profession; the need for and the incentive to change; and the lack of necessary material resources, to name just a few.

At the time Al Shanker observed in one of his famous New York Times' **Where We Stand** columns, "There is a backlash against the idea of public education controlled by the government in these newly free Eastern European countries. For more than 40 years, public education meant Communist-controlled education. And many still argue that if you want to make sure your kids don't get an education full of propaganda, you should set up private schools, or better yet, religious schools, because these were banned under the Communists."

And, in fact, Poland is moving in exactly this direction. It established a policy of subsidizing 50 percent of a student's tuition at private schools. They hoped to stimulate private investors and churches, and groups of teachers, to create new, independent private schools. In the early 1990s such schools began sprouting up all over Poland. Even former Solidarity leaders who were now in high-level administrative positions in the Ministry of Education believed that this approach was the **only** way to stimulate the growth and development of new approaches to teaching and learning. This was because these schools, free from the suspect history of the tainted schools, would not be bound by the rules and regulations and set the curriculum of the state. This, they thought, was the only way to generate models of innovation and experimentation for the country.

I argued with my new friends about this approach, explaining how we in the United States have traditionally viewed our public schools as the foundation of our democracy. I described the fears of supporters of US public education of a growing class system of rich and poor schools being the outcome of efforts here to "privatize" schools. I didn't make any converts. My new Polish colleagues remained convinced that the necessary changes in their schools were impossible within the state system.

My point about the state supporting private schools that might teach intolerance or hatred did not impress Marec. "Unlike the U.S.," he said, "we do not have such extremist groups. Maybe a few, but not that many that they are listened to. Besides," he continued, "the state would still have some say over these schools."

I thought it was easy for him to say such groups don't exist now, when they allowed no groups of any kind to exist in Communist Poland. I had just read a disturbing front-page newspaper account the previous day in the *International Herald Tribune*. It read "*Anti-Semitism Without Jews*," a story about the resurgence of anti-Semitism in this country with less than 10,000 Jews. As one philosopher observed, he who does not know history is destined to repeat it.

While Poland's needs are vastly different from ours, how their school system is reshaped will determine the direction of their country. Having the state support a network of private schools, with the potential for perpetuating nationalistic or religious or other kinds of beliefs, especially in the tinderbox of transition, could ultimately undermine the very democracy they are trying to achieve. As we have seen with the end of totalitarianism, a resurgence of nationalism, prejudice and hatred has occurred in several of these fledgling democracies, especially in the Balkans. These feelings are outgrowths of the economic frustrations the people feel as prices skyrocket and paychecks shrink or vanish altogether. An ignorant and frustrated populace takes out its anger and disillusionment over the agonizingly slow pace of change. Public schools, with their potential to transmit shared values, might mitigate against some dangerous divisions.

When I asked these Teacher Solidarity activists what the biggest problem facing education in Poland was, they didn't hesitate to say it was the attitude of teachers. This was, they explained, because even those teachers who were committed to teaching, learned to teach through lecture and drill and rote memorization. So even if they did want to change education, and these activists believed that many of them didn't, they wouldn't know how to do it. My new friends also firmly believed that not only the content of what was taught had to change, but the way it was taught also had to change.

Much of the reason for these concerns dealt with the previous systematic elimination of the nation's intelligentsia. "The old regime kept teacher salaries so low and working conditions so poor that a kind of negative selection occurred," said Marec, the Solidarity spokesperson and former teacher. "This eliminated the gifted and talented, so that only the least able people, those who couldn't find any other job, went into teaching. Except, of course, for some fans of the job." He then smiled, for he had been one of that latter group.

Besides impoverished salaries and miserable working conditions, there was no tradition of professional growth for teachers. Once qualified, or pseudo-qualified, there was no expectation for them to continue their own educations. As a result, Polish teachers were unaware of new and innovative teaching strategies and methodologies. There was no system of teacher evaluation, so there was no accountability. Most Polish teachers have no knowledge of cutting-edge practices and approaches which could help them teach children to think critically and creatively. Forging a new Poland through education remains a dream, harbored by the committed few who are not afraid of the work required to invent it all.

"You would have to be crazy to want to do that," exclaimed Marec. He was responding to the pressing need for innovation, experimentation and reform of both the content and the process of teaching. "You would have to create everything, absolutely everything! You would have to work night and day, so much time to invent lessons, find books and materials. No! No! No! You would have to be crazy to do that."

Fortunately, not all teachers feel that way. Isabella and her colleagues were taking immediate advantage of the new freedom and creating an interdisciplinary curriculum for their high school students, combining art, history, and literature. They planned to work together and support each other in trying out their new ideas.

I asked Isabella if she and her colleagues would share their ideas and lessons with teachers across Poland if they are successful. She laughed and said, "Well, maybe outside our region here. However, we want to make our school the best in this whole region, so we would share only with those teachers outside it!"

This intense woman, who, with her peers is trying to create a new vision of schooling, also spends most of her spare time at the union office. Here, the union's goals are posted on newsprint all around the room. These goals included building the union's membership and improving the nation's education. Like many union activists, Isabella says her work is hard on her family, as, in following her professional beliefs, she spends too little time with them.

Other problems emerged in our conversation. As the decentralization of decision-making occurs across Poland, the issue of some form of shared decision making in schools is a natural question. Yet what would happen in those schools where the majority are from the old "official" union? As Al Shanker noted in his column, for more than 40 years they fired teachers with the wrong views. "Should all the hacks who are now on the faculty be fired? Would that violate their academic freedom? And if they stay and the schools get to run their own affairs, doesn't that amount to turning them over to the Communist-appointed faculties?"

The potential for backlash also exists among some Solidarity members. I shuddered when I heard one Solidarity member describe an agreement his local union was trying to secure with local school officials. This agreement would allow Solidarity to reject the hiring of any teacher they objected to because of his or her political beliefs.

Ironically, as the union grew in power and influence, Solidarity leaders were being brought into positions of authority in the government. This left voids in its own leadership ranks. Gryzina, now the Vice-minister for Education, is an example. She is the former president of the Wroclaw Teacher Solidarity, the place known as the heart of Teacher Solidarity in Poland. The person who replaced her as the local union president has priorities far different from hers. She was obviously pained at this change of priority in an organization that she had worked underground in for more than a decade. She was torn over the responsibilities she assumed for running the new government.

Gryzina had another, quite different and quite unexpected problem in this new position. Not only was she not a Solidarity member anymore, but some of her biggest problems in her new position came from, of all places, Solidarity members themselves. It seems that, just as in the olden days when the party controlled officials, some Solidarity members seemed to think that they should be able to control her!

And what about schools in the United States, my Polish hosts wanted to know. "We have told you that our major problems are teaching children about democracy, about thinking for themselves; about motivating teachers to reform and innovate with teaching; and giving teachers a greater say in running our schools. What are your problems?"

I was embarrassed to admit to them that after 200 years of democracy, our own problems included how to teach our children about democracy and how to think for themselves. They included how to encourage teachers to take the lead in school reform, and how to give teachers greater say in what happens in their schools. How could this be? I asked myself. While it was true that we are not dealing with party hacks and textbooks full of lies, the parallels between the American and the Polish experiences were disturbing to me.

For sadly, shamefully, many of our children in the United States do not know how to think effectively for themselves. To be sure, the situation is less desperate in the high-income suburbs than in the low-income certain-city neighborhoods. Study after study concurs that while we may be doing a better job getting all students to a floor-level proficiency in the 3 Rs. However, we may be doing so at the expense of the skills that count the most in this complex and changing world. I thought back to the famous "A *Nation at Risk*" study of 1983 and of its ominous warning of a rising tide of mediocrity. I remembered its bold assertion that if another country had attempted to do to us what we are doing to ourselves we would consider it a unilateral act of war. Certainly a flurry of activity has resulted since then, but has it been radical enough to stave off an act of war?

Perhaps we never took this warning seriously because we, too, are the products of our own system, a system that has taught us that we are the best. Many people do not believe the continuing international comparisons showing our decline. We do not believe that our international competitiveness is eroding, that our urban infrastructure is crumbling, that the gap between rich and poor is widening. We do not want to believe these things. But could we afford to ignore the warning signals of decline?

And so, too many of our children continue to attend underfunded, overcrowded, command-and-control style urban schools with a one-size-fits-all modus operandi. Everything that happens in those schools is driven by a frenzy to raise scores on standardized tests. Often these tests cannot yet measure the real survival skills of the future—thinking for a living, inferring meaning from complex material, solving problems with multiple steps, defending a point of view, communicating well and getting along with others. We can't expect these things to be learned in an institution designed primarily to teach basic literacy, can we? In many ways I think that we are just like the Poles. We have to face the fact that our schools, especially our urban schools, must be totally reinvented to serve vastly different purposes than those they were initially designed to serve.

Here I was, with these brave people, people who valued freedom and democracy enough to go to jail for it. They, and thousands like them, knew coercion, fear, harassment, and martial law. Yet they endured. They were controlled, but never really owned. The Communist regime's efforts to keep them docile and subservient only succeeded in making them strong and resilient. And now they have their freedom. Here they were, sitting before me, talking about their future, full of hope, eagerly searching for ways to move forward with their important work. And I was humbled, as rarely before or since.

Joanna's mother had made the dinner for us, a delicious meal of tomato soup, potatoes, pork chops, cole slaw, vegetable salad, wine, and dessert and coffee. When I asked why they were doing all of this to mark my visit, they said simply that it was because they are Polish.

August 1, 1990

It was my last day in Wroclaw. Gryzina picked me up at 3:00 to take me on another adventure. This time out in the country to a town called Minich for a day in the life of the new vice-minister of Education. She wanted to show me a typical day in her new job supervising thousands of school employees. The first stop was a visit to the teacher's "rest home." I thought they were taking me to a nursing home for teachers, but it turned out to be a state-supported resort area, with some housing allocated for teachers. The resort had several hundred detached and semidetached cottages, a swimming pool, and other grounds for sports and activities.

It seems that in Poland there is a social department in the education ministry. Teachers apply to come to these resorts with their families, and the state pays part of the costs. I wondered if this were another example of perks for party members. My hosts proudly showed off the resort, expressing bewilderment that my country didn't provide such opportunities for its teachers. I didn't want to tell them that U.S. teachers wouldn't even want to come here because back home the place would be considered substandard. And from what I could see, the teacher' section (each worker-type had a different section) was the worst section of all. We then went to visit a local four-room schoolhouse. This building was new, with a spanking new gymnasium. The astonishment and envy expressed by my traveling partners were amazing. They deeply regretted that their own children did not have access to something so wonderful. How much we take for granted in the U.S.

Anna had invited me to her name day (or birthday) party on my last evening in Wroclaw. I brought a bottle of vodka and was glad to find that four or five people at the party spoke English. I had a fine time, but unexpectedly, I found myself on the 11:15 p.m. train at evening's end.

It seems that the Wroclaw Hotel had made my reservation for an 8:20 a.m. flight on Saturday. They didn't tell me, though, that I had to buy my ticket at the Lot Airlines office in town. Naively assuming that I could simply show up at the airport and buy my ticket, I learned at the party that this was impossible. The only way to make my connection and get back to Warsaw was by train.

Marec drove me to the train station and helped me get a berth on the train. He probably had to give the conductor some money, for he let me on the train without a ticket, because, of course, the train station was closed, too. I got a bunk and slept my way to Warsaw, arriving at 6:30 a.m. It was very interrupted sleep, as the train jolted to its stops and starts and rumbled along the tracks. It was a comfortable, but eerie feeling to be speeding through Poland in the middle of the night. I heard a strange language being called out in the dark at each stop, the coughing of my fellow passengers. There was no way to communicate with anyone except by pointing. I survived nicely.

August 2, 1990

On my last day in Poland I walked around Warsaw, since I hadn't spent much time there earlier. I sat sipping coffee in its Market Square, trying to absorb a bit of the history of this city which had been completely bombed in the war. Just rubble and ruins at war's end, this section had been renovated to its former character and architecture. How despondent the Poles must have been to return (those lucky enough to return) from banishment to these ruins. And what grit and stamina to start their cities, and their lives, all over again. Now there are shops and schools and children and flowers everywhere.

Our children don't learn to think for themselves well, I thought, but too many of them also don't care. I recall U.S. teachers describing the bewilderment of their students at their emotional reaction to the dismantling of the Berlin Wall. They couldn't place the events of Eastern Europe in any context, let alone the one needed to appreciate the importance of them. They couldn't relate what was happening to their own lives. They quoted one student as saying, "I'm sorry, but what is this talk of satellites? Are we talking about satellite dishes or what?" They attributed the confusion and apathy to many causes—the students' busy lives of school and work, with little time for any thing else; to the fact that few read newspapers or magazines; to their parent' own lack of interest in these events; and to the perceived irrelevance of such earthshaking events.

We lecture our students. Bemoan their apathy. Plead with them to care. But do we care ourselves? Do we know enough to care? We teachers, parents, community and political leaders must constantly remember our duty to transmit to the next generation the values that hold us together as a nation. Our public schools are the only institution that can transmit the values that bind us as a society. In some senses, the reason our children don't think, don't care, and don't appreciate these values is the way our schools are structured. Doesn't learning to understand, respect, and appreciate ideas, knowledge and values happen when these things are made real for children? When they live and breathe and experience democratic ideas and problems that have relevance to their lives? When they are actively engaged in grappling with, arguing about, debating over real problems?

This kind of learning requires brave and courageous teaching. Such teaching requires the most passionate, skilled, knowledgeable teachers we can find. Teachers who can think for themselves and whose professional judgment and autonomy are valued and respected. For teaching the children, here and also in Poland, is our most important work. We must break the cycle of complacency. As Robert Hutchins once said, "The death of democracy is not likely to be an assassination or ambush. It will be a slow extinction from apathy, indifference and undernourishment."

I don't think we can afford to lose our freedom to gain an appreciation of it. We must find another way. My way was to go to Poland to see for myself what was going on. The journey expanded my knowledge, understanding, and appreciation of the fight for freedom. Again, I realized that I must continue to learn more about history and the world, and never forget.

My week had been eye-opening, exciting, and provocative. I had met some great people and saw a Poland that few in the free world have ever seen. But it was the second week, the week that I was moved and was touched by the real Polish experience that meant the most to me. I was touched by the kindness and generosity of people who didn't even know me, people who didn't have a lot to give themselves. Gryzina's last words to me as I was leaving were, "Now you have friends here in Poland."

Chapter VI.
The CTU Years, 1992-95:
Quest For Union Leadership

After eight years away, I was home again. During that time my parents had moved and the CTU office had moved, and, of course, I had moved. So it was the same and very different. But it was home. I was back. But back to what?

Something else had changed. During my absence, in 1988, in frustration with the quality of Chicago's school system, the Illinois legislature had passed a school reform law that received national attention. Many other school districts around the country had been experimenting with various forms of school-based management. Dade County, Florida, for example, and Rochester, New York, all in cooperation with the teachers' unions. This new Illinois law, however, was markedly different from earlier school based management (SBM) efforts. The legislation was influenced heavily by the vocal Chicago reform community, which was made up of leaders of various community-based organizations that wanted a say over the schools. The law radically changed the power dynamics in Chicago schools. In one fell swoop, it decentralized the command and control hierarchy of the Board of Education's central office. It gave "power to the people," so to speak. To the people, however, not to the teachers.

Now, instead of one-size-fits-all decisions imposed unquestioningly on the schools from the top down, new Local School Councils (LSC) were established to make decisions at the school level. LSCs had the unprecedented power to hire and fire the principals and to approve the school's school improvement plan (SIP). Each LSC was to consist of 11 members, including the principal, two teachers, and eight parents and community members. And, unlike the other SBM experiments, the Chicago Teacher Union—the CTU—was not involved in the development of the plan. The CTU neither supported nor opposed the legislation.

Nor did the union play any role at all in this dramatic and drastic reform of the Chicago Public Schools. That lack of participation showed. Teachers had only two votes out of 11 on these new LSCs. The legislation did include a provision for the establishment in each school of what it called the PPAC, the Professional Personnel Advisory Committee, which was supposed to advise the LSC. Teachers and other school workers knew pretty quickly what kind of power that meant. They knew from experience that advice and input were code words for powerlessness.

I wondered why the CTU and its state affiliate, the Illinois Federation of Teachers (IFT), chose to remain silent, given the implications of the new law. Perhaps they thought opposing the legislation would make the union look bad. Perhaps the leadership thought, as some teachers did, that two voices on the LSC were more than teachers had before reform. Perhaps they thought that these majority-parent councils would listen to the professionals and take their advice, or that the LSCs wouldn't really make any difference anyway.

John was a top aide to now-President Vaughn (Assistant for Educational Issues) by this time. He felt that the CTU had to play a role in the implementation of the 1988 reform law. He believed that the two teachers on the LSC, which had to be elected by the teachers in their buildings, could play an important leadership role. They could advance teachers' agendas, and the union's agenda, if they were informed and supported in that role. The CTU did hold a few workshops for these teacher-LSC members on issues such as how to read a school budget or write a school improvement plan. But the CTU never really embraced these members as an extension of the union's own leadership.

Yet the possibility for teacher leadership within the 1988 reform umbrella did exist. John thought that perhaps the knowledge, expertise and experience of CTU-LSC members could influence the kinds of things that were decided in their schools. I suspect this possibility motivated John as we worked our way through the many drafts of our MacArthur proposal. He believed in teacher leadership and in the union's responsibility to nurture it. And he thought that the CTU Quest Center could be the union's way to identify, nurture and support such leadership.

I remember the first time I went to my new office in the CTU headquarters in Chicago's Merchandise Mart Plaza. The old CTU offices had been on a couple of small, cramped floors in an ancient office building on Wells Street, with el trains rattling nearby. These new offices reflected the corporate world. The Mart itself is an imposing edifice sitting on the Chicago River. It has the feel of an impenetrable fort, or even like a moated castle, almost out of reach. The CTU was still renting, although this time in the "high rent" district. Jacqui Vaughn's proposal to buy a building had been rejected as too expensive.

The grant John and I had written called for the creation of a center for teacher leadership on school reform, a center within the CTU. We knew that we had to give this center a special name, since a name says so much. After exploring many possibilities, we decided on the Quest Center. We wanted to suggest a journey. We wanted to express our desire to invite people to join in this journey, or quest, for radically improved schools and dramatically improved student learning. We both had heard Al Shanker's warning about the future of public education if the schools didn't change, and we both heard the clock ticking. We didn't have time for evolutionary change. We needed revolutionary change. *Now.*

The Quest Center, while an official part of the CTU, had two bodies which were to guide its direction. The first was a Governing Board, almost a misnomer because in reality it acted as more of an advisory board, and a group of "National Advisors." The Governing Board was made up, not surprisingly, of a majority of CTU members. It also included representation from the Board of Education, the State Board of Education, and influential community groups. We believed that these non-union partners had important things to tell us and also that their support of our efforts was important, too.

We had a press conference to announce to the world the MacArthur grant and the new CTU initiative. I started in February and they held the press conference in February. Jacqui Vaughn, Al Shanker and Peter Martinez of the MacArthur Foundation were the scheduled speakers. Jacqui opened the press conference by noting the irony that there were many fewer press people than usual at a CTU press conference for a good news story.

"We can now begin to look at education reform," she began. "We have spent much time talking about school reform, governance, who will be making the decisions. Now it's time for the educators who will be implementing programs to have a say about what is being done."

One reporter asked her how the CTU had come to submit such a proposal to the MacArthur Foundation in the first place. Her response was telling.

"We know our system need improving. We want our students ready for the next century. So we went to the corporate and philanthropic community and convinced them that as unionists, teachers and educators, we not only are concerned about our salaries and working conditions, but also about what happens in the classroom and our ability to do that which is expected of us and to which we are committed to doing."

Al Shanker spoke next. "This is a very important step and a very unique step," he said. "Chicago is the only major city in the country that will be developing the capacity of teachers to be involved in school reform and school change. What we've had so far are reforms that don't connect with teachers and schools...I wouldn't be surprised if the

Clinton administration picked it up as a model…If reform is going to succeed, it will be because of programs like this."

Al Shanker was one of the Quest Center's national advisors. The national advisors were another important piece of our plan. These 20 advisors included many movers and shakers in the national school reform debate. It included Al Shanker, Ted Sizer of the Coalition of Essential Schools, Linda Darling Hammond of Teachers College, my friends and former AFT coworkers Eugenia Kemble and Lovely Billups, Phil Schlecty, and Adam Urbanski of the Rochester Teachers Association, and my former professor, Bruce McPherson of the University of Illinois at Chicago, among others. We felt that having our work informed by, guided by and evaluated by educators of such national stature was essential. They could hold our feet to the fire about quality, perspective and credibility.

In the grant proposal, we promised that the Quest Center would have three main functions: first, it was intended to be a city wide catalyst to generate discussion, debate and interest in school reform and restructuring our schools. Like casting out a net, we wanted to hold seminars and conferences and workshops, and find those teachers and school workers who were already trying reforms and making a difference. We also were looking for those who were ready to move forward with various reforms. We wanted to bring them together to share ideas and innovations and multiply the number of CTU members who were taking the lead in reforms at the school level.

Our initial conference was held in the third month of the Quest Center's existence. It was called *"Restructuring Our Schools"*. Since the CTU had never done anything like this before, we didn't know how many people, if any, would show up. Yet we had high hopes and booked a big room at the Merchandise Mart for the opening session. More than three hundred and fifty members came. We were ecstatic. The calls and registration forms kept coming and coming and coming. It turned out that the room we had reserved barely held all of the attendees, and many breakout workshop sessions were standing-room-only. It was wonderful. We built it, and they came. It was more than encouraging that there were so many members out there resonating to a call from their union to take part in the dialogue of change. These members saw themselves as possible change agents. The Quest Center was christened and we were on our way.

Our second function was to offer a competitive request for proposals (RFP) initiative. We would put out a call each year for the most exciting, innovative plans for school reform. The best would receive an incentive grant to spur ideas. There was the possibility of additional monies if proposed reforms bore fruit in increased student achievement. The proposals had to be teacher-developed and include sign-off by the school's union representative (called "delegates" in the CTU), by the administration and the LSC. The Quest Center's Governing Board selected the 10 best proposals in the first year. It picked the 15 best in years two and three, for a total of 40 schools in three years of the MacArthur grant.

The third function we hoped to serve was to be a clearinghouse of resources for school people interested in learning more about school reform. This included the research, and the models of school reform, and information on the pitfalls and the possibilities. We had a resource library of books, articles, audiotapes and videotapes which teams could borrow or come in and use.

We also arranged for a course called *"Restructuring Our Schools,"* to be offered with graduate credit through the University of Illinois at Chicago. It was an independent study course for teams of teachers in a school. In other words, members could only take the course if a team of three or more teachers signed up together to take the class. Once enrolled, a team received a course syllabus which included dozens of possibilities for each course topic. A team would design its own course of study, based on the dozens of activities listed under each topic, and based on the unique needs and issues of the team and the school in which team members worked.

The idea for this course came out of some careful listening to Al Shanker's speeches. In one I was intrigued to hear him point to the Boy Scout model of hands-on project learning. He described how for each badge or level, Scouts had to accomplish certain things and show them to a parent or leader. Could we design school learning like this, he asked? I thought that model might work well for teachers wishing to customize their course of study of certain reform/restructuring topics around various kinds of hands-on learning activities. Teams would have to go to a school and observe a certain practice, or read an article and discuss it, or view a video and write a critique. They had to choose the projects and turn in some kind of written evidence, signed by all of the members, that the project was complete.

The final, culminating project of the course (and the only time that team members had to show up at CTU headquarters after the course introduction), was a team presentation. Teams had to share their jointly developed ideal plan for school change (whether or not they could ever really implement it). The plan had to be based on the ideas and models they studied in the course. Hundreds of teachers, in dozens of Chicago schools, began reading and studying and exploring reform. They journeyed to other schools and school systems looking for better ways to reach and teach their students. It was exciting to see that much interest and involvement.

Many plans presented to us did result in formal proposal submissions for Quest grants and grants from other entities funding schools. There were many thoughtful, informed proposals. Many were innovative and exciting. Many were good starts needing to be refined. Many needed work. Things were percolating. People were reading, talking, debating, and coming to the CTU office with proposals to change and improve their schools.

On the other hand, almost from the start, tensions emerged. One of the first signals I received was when I went to the CTU's head of communications. I asked about doing a press release on the press conference announcing the MacArthur grant and the Quest Center.

Instead of asking me about the event and taking down the details, which is how things were done at the AFT, she handed me a scrap of paper with the fax number of the PR Newswire. I was told to do it myself.

There was some grumbling among some CTU officers and staff members about being controlled by "outsiders," i.e. the MacArthur Foundation. There were some comments about professional issues not having any place in the union. There was a contract waiver clause in the CTU contract, which meant that the CTU agreed to the issue. Yet there was resentment at our efforts to assist members in getting waivers from the contract when they wanted to try certain reforms. Modifying the start of the school day and accumulating minutes each month for half days of staff development, for example. There were also some school delegates who had been left out of proposal planning discussions at their schools and then who, understandably, refused to sign the school-based proposals.

There were some delegates who didn't like the particular changes that planning team members wanted and who complained to CTU staff. For example, there was a team of teachers from Taft High School that received a Quest grant for starting a small school, an initiative. It turned out, however, that the plan was being mandated by the principal for the entire school. Taft's principal had requested to be on the Quest Center's Governing Board and he was appointed. Taft's delegate, a CTU activist and member of the CTU Executive Board, also was on the Quest Center Governing Board. But the majority of Taft's teachers didn't want anything to do with small schools. They weren't happy with the Quest Center for the recognition we brought their school for something that they didn't want. So we heard about it.

John's favorite saying at the time was "Real change is real hard."

We all expected growing pains and conflicts as a result of encouraging and supporting change. Not everyone wants to change, and even those that do want change get discouraged. But the tension in the CTU offices had less to do with the challenges of changing schools and more to do with egos. While some of this was the legitimate grappling with a new role for the union, much of it was a grappling for power. Many insiders resented John. I didn't realize how much until the infamous 1993 CTU staff retreat.

John carried baggage from decades before when he was a leader in the union's opposition. He had even run for CTU president once, in the early 1970s. The then CTU president Robert Healy had brought John on staff in 1974, perhaps to co-opt him. John was smart, savvy and even threatening to the less secure around him. Under Healy, John had been a CTU Field Representative. Once Jacqui Vaughn took over as CTU president, John was promoted to Director of the Field Reps and then Assistant to the President for Educational Issues. Most important, he had Jacqui's ear.

So, of course, many in the inner sanctum hoped John would fail, fearing that the better he (or his initiatives) looked, the worse they looked. The sabotage that was under the surface for the most part erupted at the CTU staff retreat held in 1993 at a resort. John had been asked to develop the agenda and, as it turned out, it set him up for disaster. Some wondered what he would make them talk about? Why he was the one picked to do the agenda? Why Jacqui had asked him to do it and not them?

Some tension was our own fault; I realized that at the retreat. Our rhetoric of transforming the system intimidated many inside the union, for if the system changed, then wouldn't the union have to change with it? Veteran CTU leadership and staff considered that taking advantage of the contract by adopting a waiver for a reform initiative was somehow anti-union. We were talking about issues that were out of the realm of many CTU officers and staff, just as their issues were not in our areas of expertise.

I don't think the Quest staff ever thought or said that what they were doing in the union wasn't as important as what we were doing. We did believe we were serving the union membership in a different way, but not necessarily in a better or worse way.

There we were at the retreat. I had much experience leading seminars, both in my AFT work with teachers and for five years at my local library in Washington, D.C. So John asked me to lead a discussion on an article called "What Should Unions Do?" written by John Hoerr and printed in the Harvard Business Review. This article raised questions about the role of and future of unions in today's contemporary America. Hoerr discussed the decline of unionism but advanced the idea that while a particular kind of adversarial unionism may be obsolete, unionism per se is not. He said that unions don't have to be obstacles to competitiveness and success. Unions can make stronger companies; they can be a surprisingly effective means of integrating employees into decision making. In short, unions needed to reinvent themselves in changing times, much as companies were trying to do.

John and I had thought that reading and discussing this article together, and exploring any comparisons to education, might stimulate an interesting and productive discussion. Some colleagues thought differently. Jacqui left the retreat after the opening session. Then the gloves came off.

The seminar leader usually throws out a question meant to elicit discussion and while I can't remember what the question was, I'll never forget the first answer.

"What are we reading this kind of stuff for? Did you see where it was published? What in the world can we ever get out of a piece published in the Harvard Business Review?" Tom Reece, who was then CTU Vice-president, asked disparagingly.

It was all downhill after that. What do you expect from our schools, given the kinds of students that attend them? What do you mean "reach out to the business community"—why would we ever want to do that? What do you mean the union has to change? These were the kinds of responses to the questions for discussion developed for the various small group sessions. Most of the sessions I participated in could only be described as hostile. No one thought that questions about the role of the union in a time of great change were necessary. Why do we need to talk about this, the staff seemed to be asking. Just continue to do what we always do. To them it seemed a no-brainer. They didn't think the discussion was relevant, and they resented John, who had organized the retreat this way, and the perceived implication that they were doing something wrong.

At one point I accused the man who asked what they could expect of the schools given the quality of Chicago's students of being a racist. It was that ugly and continued back at the office. When we all returned to work, a few of us found anonymous "It's the members, stupid" signs (remember the "It's the economy, stupid" presidential slogan?) on our office doors. That retreat was talked about for months, which drifted into years.

I now think that two things were happening. The resentment of John that would have been there no matter how he had organized the retreat or what kinds of questions were asked. The people who were threatened by John did not want him to have any new or extra authority or any "power" over them. I guess I don't blame anyone who feels threatened by an implication, real or imagined, that they are somehow doing something wrong. The other realization for me was that the "us verses them" mentality was the result of a genuine belief that the union didn't need to change. Maybe the entire world around it was changing, the economy, the schools, even the members. Yet there was a significant group of CTU staff and leadership which truly did not see those changes as having any implications for the union. It truly believed in a "this too shall pass" mentality. The union had survived outside changes before, and it would again. Unfortunately, unknown to many of us, Jacqui was too sick from breast cancer to challenge and counter this thinking.

Personal tragedy struck my family again in 1992. My only sister Barb, a beautiful, kind and generous woman of 33, was killed, a victim of domestic violence. We were stunned and stupefied. We were completely unaware of any big problems or previous domestic abuse. Like many victims, she didn't tell anyone. Now, again, my parents had to bury another child, my brothers and I another sibling. Yet this time, we had not only our grief, but three babies to think about.

With my family behind me, despite being a single, working woman, the courts gave me custody of Barb's children, who at the time were 1, 3 and five years old. I immediately moved from my new condo in the city to a rented house in the suburbs to be near my family members, for their sustenance and support. It was that family connection that helped us *all* make it through that nightmare of grief and loss and helplessness. I was able to adopt these cherished children. Now we could really try to move on with our lives. Becoming and being their mom has been one of the most wonderful things that has ever happened to me. Another door always seems to open, especially when life seems bleak most.

Initially my plan was to quit working and live on my AFT severance pay and whatever was available from the estate. Surprisingly, my parents told me that I should not have to set aside my career and that they wanted to help in raising the children. John also was horrified at my talk of resigning, barely four months after the Quest Center had opened its doors. He and Jacqui Vaughn offered me their support for a flex time arrangement. The arrangement included three ten-hour days in the office, during which time my parents would care for the children. I literally worked from 7:30 a.m. when I stepped on the train to 5:30 p.m. when I stepped off it. The other two days were half-days working at home, where I had a computer and fax machine to keep me connected. I worked at home while the children were in half-day preschool and kindergarten.

As with the loss of Jimmy, a focus on work helped me try to move on. My commitments to the Quest Center were strong, and slowly I was able to put my full energies into our mission. Despite the negativity that resulted from the retreat which, in fact, only erupted there, we were on a roll. Hundreds of CTU members were turning out regularly for our events, which included fall and spring conferences and ongoing courses. Every June, dozens of schools would compete for our minigrants to launch their school change efforts.

John and I were participating regularly in school reform conversations and coalitions that were happening around the city. We worked with groups like the City wide Coalition for School Reform, the Consortium on Chicago School Research, the Small Schools Coalition and Small Schools Workshop, the Annenberg Board and others. Through those exchanges, the CTU was starting to be seen as a reform participant, as an entity that had something important to contribute. Some of the "reform groupies" could see that John and I were sincere about school reform. There were questions about whether the full CTU leadership was truly embracing it.

John and I became excited about the growing national interest in setting standards for what students should know and be able to do at various points in their education. The math teachers had paved new ground when the National Council of Teachers of Mathematics published its new standards for what students needed to know. Other fields were planning their own statements about what students should know, and Al Shanker was a strong advocate for national standards. John and I could see the value in having a common set of standards to guide instruction, especially given the transience of so many of Chicago's students. We wondered whether Chicago's teachers could get in on the ground floor of the discussion (and debate) about what our students should know and be able to do. So we approached the MacArthur Foundation and the Joyce Foundation about some additional support for a standards' initiative. We wanted classroom teachers to be able to examine all the efforts underway to define the standards for various subject areas. Then they could establish a working set of standards for Chicago students. The standards could then be discussed and debated and improved upon with widespread participation from all affected by them—teachers, students, parents, business and community leaders.

It turned out that the Board of Education had advanced a similar idea. So the two foundations told us that they would only pay for such an initiative if the Board and the Union worked together on it. Jacqui Vaughn and the then-superintendent agreed and so we hammered out a plan and a process of working together that was unprecedented in Chicago. John as Assistant to the CTU President for Educational Issues and Adrienne Bailey, Deputy Superintendent for the Chicago Public Schools were co-chairs of the project. Yes, equal footing. Each decision made along the way had to have the agreement of both sides. If there was to be a twenty-person sub-committee, then each side recommended ten of them. We operated on a consensus and it was a rare and heady experience.

We had called the Council on Basic Education in from Washington, D.C., an organization that advocated strong standards, to provide information and technical support. We launched the Chicago standards-setting effort that continues to this day. We knew that setting a set of common standards was only the first step. Professional development for the staff in teaching to the new (and higher) standards would be essential. Prior Chicago Public School reform efforts had failed because there was little attention or resources devoted to the implementation stage. We knew that if the staff didn't understand the rationale for the standards, didn't have a say in setting them, and didn't have the training or resources to teach to them, it would all be a waste of time.

The other big issue for us was the assessment system that would be used to assess whether the teachers were teaching and the students were meeting the new standards. There had been ongoing criticisms of the current standardized assessment efforts because too often there was no match between what was taught and what was tested. We didn't object to accountability if it was fair accountability. We wanted the Board of Education to adopt standards and an assessment system aligned to those standards so that there was that match.

Another part of our grant was to support teachers in creating lesson plans and teaching units aligned to our standards as models for other teachers to use. We could pay teams of teachers from various schools who worked together in developing trying out and refining standards-driven units. We published their work. We had a fierce and fundamental belief that teachers, union members, should be central to this kind of thinking and development and that part of the role of their union was to be equal partners with management on educational issues. However, difficult times were close, as death intervened.

Jacqui Vaughn lost her fight against breast cancer and died in January 1994. I've never seen such a wake. Hundreds, perhaps thousands, came by to pay her their last respects. For hours and hours they came, hot shots and dignitaries, and most of all, CTU members. She was a leader, a role model, and an inspiration for so many. Now, at the relatively young age of 55, this proud, black, teacher' union leader had left us.

Nine months later John died of a sudden heart attack. He was in his mid-fifties, too. John had had open heart surgery at age 39, and he seemed in such good, fit condition, so his death was a real shock. I lost one of my best friends the day he died. He had taught me so much. He left so quickly. It took a few days for the office to change his voice mail message. I found myself just calling his number those few days, to hear his voice again. I was already starting to forget the sound of that voice that I always enjoyed hearing at the other end of the line.

With Jacqui and John both gone, I wondered what would happen at the CTU. I waited and waited and waited. And the problem was that nothing happened. Jacqui's vice-president, Tom Reece, had taken over as president when she died and succeeded her in the officer election that occurred four months after her death. The Quest Center went on as usual, even getting new, expensive offices for our staff which now consisted of four professional staff members including me, and two support staff members. The three assistant directors had been working out of temporary carrels for years, and now they had a place to call home.

Which reminds me of one of the first staff meetings Tom Reece presided over. Sometime during the meeting, he asked all of us Quest Center staff members to stand up and pronounced us all part of the CTU. We then sat down and the meeting went on from there. I'm still not sure why he did that. Perhaps he was trying to say that we should let the retreat bygones be bygones. Perhaps he was sending a message that with John now gone, the rest of us were finally going to be considered real CTU staff members. Many of the staff had never considered us "real" union staff members. The MacArthur money had paid our salaries, and we focused on the "professional" issues, not bread and butter. Yet we had considered ourselves real CTU staff members all along.

I kept waiting. Waiting for some statement, some action, some plan that said to the world "We are here and we have something to say. We are a force to be reckoned with." Nothing happened. It was as if the reform attitude of the CTU disappeared off the face of the earth.

Before John died, I had asked him about Tom's leadership. "Let's give him a chance," he said. John worked inside the CTU system and didn't challenge it, though he remained a thorn in the side of those whom his ideas and his influence threatened. It was Jacqui who had promoted John and made him assistant to the president. I asked John whether he had any thoughts about running for union office again, especially after a year of silence from Tom Reece. John wanted to give Tom a chance. He also felt too far removed from the membership. He realized, rightly, that anyone running for union office had to have a base of support among the membership.

Meanwhile, a big legislative coup was brewing in Springfield. In the spring of 1995 the Illinois legislature essentially gave control of the school system to the mayor. It also, however, stripped the CTU of its rights to bargain over many issues such as class size, layoff procedures, seniority, privatization, among others. The once-powerful CTU could no longer bargain over these time-honored union issues. It was unbelievable.

What was even more stunning was the CTU leadership's reaction. The CTU leadership blamed the CTU *membership*! The poor members hadn't been informed by the CTU about what was coming. They had not mobilized them into a fight for their own bargaining rights. Now, according to Reece, they were the *culprits*!

Reece sent a letter to CTU delegates sent out just after the bill passed in May of 1995. In it he said, "According to the records, fewer than 15% of our 31,000 members bothered to make the effort to save their rights and their pensions...as we have found out, too many of our members do not vote, do not vote for CTU-endorsed candidates...and did not make an effort to save their job protections and their pension funding."

The union leadership was blaming the victims, when in fact, it had not informed that membership nor mobilized it to try to prevent this from happening. Here we were fighting to hold on to what we had. There was nothing on this leadership's agenda about gaining new ground. I realized that there was no vision, no interest in a vision, no hope for a vision of progressive union leadership. I started thinking about leaving.

My last summer as director of the CTU Quest Center was an exciting one. One of our earlier ideas—that of creating a union-run graduate school—looked like it might really become a reality. After our successes with the courses we were offering, combined with the challenges of the new standards initiatives, we asked ourselves whether we could develop a full-fledged masters degree curriculum. It sounded far-fetched, spectacular. But why not? We were the professionals. We knew a lot about what was needed in urban public schools and a lot about what teachers in urban public schools wanted and needed. So began the idea of the Jacqueline B. Vaughn (JBV) Graduate School for Teacher Leadership.

Once again, the MacArthur Foundation responded to our call for support for the development of the JBV Graduate School. It provided financial support for the work of a committee of experts from the public schools and the university. It supported the work of a university-experienced writer to capture our ideas and prepare our application to the Illinois Board of Higher Education for operating authority. We dreamed of a professional school dedicated to providing high quality, practitioner-oriented graduate education to practicing teachers. We said that the school would provide graduate study that:

* is driven by current research and by the best thinking about what accomplished teachers needed to know and be able to do;

* creates and supports a community of learners dedicated to developing and testing more effective ways to structure and deliver public education;

* provides students with skills, attitudes and perspectives necessary for creating and implementing visions of how public schools can contribute to the continuing development of children and communities;

* is organized around challenging standards for what students should know and be able to do in today's world.

We said that completing the program would enable students to 1) articulate a coherent, research-based vision of teaching and learning; 2) identify and describe the kind of changes necessary to realize this vision of teaching and learning; and 3) develop, carry out and evaluate strategies for change in the public schools designed to carry out the desired vision of teaching and learning. We explicitly stated that the degree would be in teacher leadership. It was not meant to be a program for teachers to get into school administration, nor would it provide courses for certification. It was meant to support teachers in what we hoped would be new roles for teachers in providing leadership for school improvement and school change.

Predictably, the local universities providing graduate programs in education screamed bloody murder. We had no right to open our own school, they said. They were already meeting the graduate needs of Chicago's teachers, they argued. One dean asked us sarcastically, "What are we supposed to do now, go out and organize teachers?"

Still, we moved ahead. Our first application to the State Board of Higher Education was rejected. It was then that we hired the consultant to help translate what we said we wanted to do into higher education language. We incorporated responses to all of the criticisms that we had received. We added all the items that the State Board told us we needed to add and resubmitted it in the summer of 1995. This whole process actually took us two years, but we kept at it. We awaited the State Board's decision.

It was the summer of 1995 when I realized that it was time to make my own decision. Jacqui was gone. John was gone. The few suggestions I had made for the CTU to do something pro active had been dismissed or ignored. For example, I had the opportunity to attend an AFT site visit to the Saturn auto plant in Spring Hill Tennessee to see up close the unique labor-management partnership they had created, something called co-management. When I got back, I suggested that the CTU go to the new Board of Education members and propose that the CTU in partnership with the Board of Education co-manage one school, or one region of the city's schools. I thought that this would be a way to prove that teachers (and their unions) weren't the cause of the problems in the schools. We could be part of the solution. I never received an answer to that memo. Soon I realized that there was never going to be any answer (or any new ideas) coming from this union leadership. So I asked myself whether I wanted to remain part of a stagnant, passive, reactive, blame-the-membership kind of union leadership. The answer was definitely not.

It was time to make a change. It was time to teach again in a public school classroom. It was time for me to try to put into practice some of the reforms I had been advocating. Perhaps it was time to go back and see first hand the impact of the reform movement at the school level. It was time to look for the union in the membership. I looked forward to regular classroom teaching again after such a long break. It turned out to be relatively easy to find a teaching position. There was a shortage of special education teachers and that was my field.

But I was ambivalent. What concerned me was whether or not once I got out there I'd find anyone else with a longing for real union leadership. I certainly knew that I did not have the base of support that John had said one needed to run for union office. But I knew people in at least the 45 Quest schools we had nurtured this far. They knew me and what I stood for over the previous three years. Maybe that was a start.

Before John died, it had never even occurred to me to run for union office. I had asked him about his interest in running, but I didn't think about it for myself. Now I felt almost compelled to think about it. Compelled by me, anyway.

Loss struck our family once again that summer. Once again, the phone call came out of the blue, completely unexpectedly. Once again, the loss was instant. My vigorous and healthy father died of a heart attack on the eighteenth hole of the golf course. Stunned, we had to face the fact that he was gone. He was 74 and, with my mother, had been helping me care for Barb's—my—children three days a week. We used to joke, he and I, about being his age and still concerned about quality preschool programs and soccer treats. He and my mom would pick up the two youngest from preschool those three days a week at 11:30 a.m., and care for them until my arrival at home at 5:30. They insisted that this was how they wanted to spend their retirement, and I was grateful for that assistance. I could throw myself into my work because I knew the kids were safe in their hands.

My dad did that for the last three years of his life. The kids have so many wonderful stories and memories of that special time with their grandparents. My dad's constant stream of jokes. The tricks he played on them. Them putting *him* in time out. Stopping at his favorite place, the Plush Horse Ice Cream Parlor for a cone. I think back about him and that time often. We all miss him so much. It was not the way he had planned his retirement, but it's hard to imagine any other retiree being as loved and needed as he was. Under the circumstances, I don't think he would have had it any other way.

Two weeks before the '95-96 school year was to begin, I was still struggling with this decision over dinner with a good friend. Somehow, as we were eating and talking—almost in the middle of a sentence—I realized that I had decided to leave. I was no longer torn between and among options. I had two weeks to put the Quest Center director's business in order for whoever would fill the position next.

The CTU leadership and top staff members seemed shocked in reacting to my decision. (They were probably just as relieved as shocked.) The PR director, the one who had told me to fax my own press release when I first got there, came to my office to ask me herself if it were really true. It was the first time she had ever come to me for anything. Tom Reece also stopped by, also a first, and thanked me for the job I had done and wished me well. I had given him my two weeks notice, simply stating that I felt that "it was time to return to the classroom and put into practice all of the things I had learned since I left it." If that meant union leadership and teacher leadership, well then, so be it.

Here I was again, stepping into the unknown. This was a different unknown. When I went to Washington and the AFT, there were people waiting for me. When I came back home to run the Quest Center, there were people waiting for me. Was there anyone out there in the schools waiting for me? I had no idea.

On my last day at the CTU Quest Center, I received a letter from the Illinois State Board of Higher Education granting us operating authority for the Jacqueline B. Vaughn Graduate School for Teacher Leadership. To this day, that operating authority has not been used by the CTU leadership. Perhaps they didn't want to go forward with my idea. Perhaps they didn't know what to do to next. Nevertheless, another exciting reform possibility has slipped away.

Chapter VII.
The Marquette years, 1995-present: Quest For Teacher Leadership

Marquette Elementary School, September 2, 1995. I reentered teaching as a teacher of students with learning disabilities. This time I *was* certified in learning disabilities and ready to see what had happened in schools and classrooms since I had left the Chicago Public schools fifteen years earlier. I also felt that it was time to "walk the education reform talk." If I believed in much of the reform rhetoric, didn't I also have a responsibility to practice what I and others had been preaching?

So I reentered the world of the Chicago Public School teacher. I was ready to apply everything I had learned since I had left teaching, as I said in my CTU resignation letter. Marquette is on Chicago's Southwest side. At the time, it served about 1,700 children, mostly poor (with 95 percent of the students qualifying for free lunch). Teachers, students, and staff were housed in one main building and a branch, a school rented from the Chicago Archdiocese. In 1995, the school had a majority of Hispanic children. Next in proportion were Black students, and then a small number of Arabic children. Only about 25 percent of the children were reading on grade level. Today the main school building has an addition, and Marquette serves over 2,000 children.

I had applied to teach at Marquette because its faculty had submitted a grant to the CTU Quest Center the previous year. The grant was for the creation of four small schools, a reform in which I strongly believed. Marquette did not get a Quest grant at the time, due simply to the tremendous number of applications that year. Yet when I found out that there was a position open there, I remembered it as a school trying to reform and so I applied. I became a member of its faculty.

Teaching in 1995, I found quickly, was deja vu all over again. I found myself conducting my LD classes in a closet. My "classroom" was literally a closet, a small room with a huge sink, situated off a regular classroom. My students and I had to cut through ongoing kindergarten classes every period to get back and forth to my room. Special education has always been seen by many special educators as the stepchild of regular education, and we learn to adapt. Still, a closet?

We made do. I was a resource teacher, which means that my students stayed in their regular classrooms most of the day. Eight kids at a time came to me from regular classrooms for two or three periods for extra support to help remediate their learning disabilities. Two other LD resource teachers taught the older students. I had younger children, which was enjoyable because by now my own children were in the primary grades. I thought I could draw on their interests and needs as I helped with my new students.

I was nervous after such a long hiatus from the classroom. Would I know what to do? Would I be able to help my students?

An unexpected boost arrived in the form of an invitation to teach part time at the University of Illinois at Chicago in its special education program. I had been an adjunct professor there while I was at the CTU Quest Center—the professor of record for our "Restructuring Our Schools" independent study course. I also had taught some of the CTU Graduate Program courses, such as Classroom Management and Introduction to Exceptional Children, long before I went to Washington. I had come to enjoy teaching and working with adults immensely.

This time the course was "Introduction to Learning Disabilities," and the timing was perfect for me. The old adage that you never know something as well as when you have to teach it to someone else held true for me. This was a perfect way for me to reenter the classroom, by sharing up-to-the-minute information on learning disabilities. I think it was helpful for my graduate students; also, many of them were practicing teachers seeking to become certified in learning disabilities. To talk by night about what I taught by day potentially would be a powerful experience for me—and hopefully my adult students. What I was doing with my own LD students, what worked, what didn't work and why, and case studies of the students and their progress became the foundation of my course.

"You do have your own materials?" I was asked that first day at Marquette by an administrator.

Not wanting to appear inadequate or unprepared, I nodded, though I had nothing. It had been 15 years, after all. I made a quick mental note to stop at the nearest Teacher's Store on the way home that day. I rejoined the ranks of those professionals who spend much of their own money for supplies for their classrooms. [Someone should add up all that Chicago teachers themselves contribute of their own money for their classrooms. The public would be shocked, amazed and impressed at how much that would be. Imagine what the totals would be for Illinois or the USA.] On a positive note, later that year, at the request of the special education case manager, all new special education programs did receive $400 for supplies. It was a start.

My students were stunning. There was Marta, a beautiful first grader who had been hit by a car and was learning disabled as a result of traumatic brain injury. You never saw her without an absolutely glowing smile. I wanted to take her home with me. Marta was one of the lucky ones. She had loving parents and a stable home. That is just so important for any child, much less a child experiencing difficulties. Many others with whom I worked were not so fortunate.

There was Joe, one of three siblings in special education in our school. All had the same mother, but different fathers. Home was with their elderly grandmother, who had taken them in when they removed them from their mother, her daughter, for drug addiction. They had been born addicted to cocaine. Each had been diagnosed as having learning disabilities and each was hyperactive, suffering from attention deficit disorder (ADD). Of course, they all were having difficulties. Their grandmother, a religious, optimistic woman, had suffered at least one heart attack, and I worried about the children if she had another.

Then there was Nicki, another lovely girl whom her grandmother was raising. Her mother was with husband (or boyfriend) number three or four and she did not want Nicki. Nicki's grandmother was in a particularly precarious position relating to Nicki's status, because mom still claimed Nicki for the public aid she received. Grandma had no real claim to her. I worried that one day mom would simply snatch her back and grandma would be helpless to do anything about it. Nicki didn't know why her mother had her four siblings with her, and not Nicki. On the Mondays after the occasional weekends with her mother, I could see a major change in this sweet, but stubborn girl.

Hannah was full of love and hugs. She greeted me each day with her radiant smile. Hannah, too, was born addicted to drugs, to heroin. She and her sister and another baby were being raised by her grandmother, also. Hannah had attention and learning problems, but she was a good girl, eager to please, and she made progress. Then, one day, she was gone, transferred out. I never saw or heard about her again. Her grandmother had a good heart, though she was a little flighty. I just hope and pray they are okay.

We had so many entire families in the special education program. The Sander family, for example, had two children in full-time self-contained special education classes. One child received resource assistance, and two more on their way to being identified as needing special education services. Their mother's drug of choice? Alcohol. These children were born with fetal alcohol syndrome and are experiencing tremendous learning, behavioral and emotional problems, a result of prenatal damage and ongoing family chaos.

The James' family also had four children at various levels of special education, two of whom had been hospitalized in psychiatric hospitals, one for depression and another for sexual aggression. They were being raised by their mother, whom they had cited for child neglect dozens and dozens of times. I saw Mary for LD services. She had been in at least four schools in her lifetime. She was in third grade. One day she was there; the next day they were all gone. The sad thing was that you never heard about these vanished children again. Not one word. You would become attached. You would work hard to help them. Then, one day they'd disappear. They never came back. No one you asked would know where they went or what happened to them. All you could do was think of them and pray silently for them.

Here is a story I wrote about Thomas; it was published in the *Chicago Tribune*. It describes some of the heartbreak and fears teachers experience.

"A Boy Named Thomas Passes Through," **Chicago Tribune**, *Sunday, May 26, 1996*

Thomas showed up in my class in November. It was the fifth or sixth move of his seven years. He had the most beautiful smile, the brightest eyes and the deepest voice. He was born with many strikes against him, but as things go, he wasn't among the worst off.

His father was in jail and his mother, who at 26 had five children, had attempted suicide several times. While not appearing to be an abused child, Thomas certainly was neglected. He was late for school and usually hungry. He wore filthy, ripped and oversized clothes. He frequently got into scuffles and other trouble around the school. But through it all, he was a carefree, happy, innocent little boy. That smile could light up your day.

I am a Chicago teacher, only one of 23,000 or so who teach the Thomases of this city. We agonize over each one and question ourselves every day about the quality of what we give to our children, knowing that the consequences mean the world to them. You might not think of us in the trenches like that, worrying about our children and trying our best to give them our best, because no one is really telling our story. No one is telling the stories of hundreds and thousands of children, 80 percent of them poor and minority, and years behind academically before they ever even reach us.

Thomas was in that group. He was placed in our "developmental" first grade and provided extra support services for children with learning disabilities (LD). I was his LD teacher. Thomas stayed with us for five months, at which time his mother just picked up and left, again, her typical response to stress. In those five months, Thomas went from being a non-reader to beginning fluency with first grade material, despite the fact that he missed 20 days of school during that period. He was curious, creative, motivated, sweet—at times a handful, but a pleasure to see each day.

As I worked with Thomas, I would think about his circumstances compared to those of my own children who are about his age. Knowing the instability of his home life, I worried about the kind of life that was in store for him. What would happen if his family continued moving, if his chronic absences kept him from making any steady progress academically and he ended up poor and uneducated, with no skills and no hope for the future? When would his innocence and curiosity turn to contempt and apathy? When would society stop thinking he was so cute and look on him with fear and loathing? I know that education is his only chance.

Stories like Thomas' seem remote but will affect us all in some way in the future. We know that for many of these children we are their only hope. We accept that responsibility as part of the territory. We also need the authority, the resources and the support of the public to be able to do the best job that we can do.

Thomas has moved again. I said good-bye to him and I felt a pang of grief because he never looked back. He walked into his future with confidence and innocence. I'm hoping for the best for him.

The teachers at Marquette were gracious from the outset. They welcomed me and made me feel at home. But after the initial welcome, I became lonely. Our school day ran from 8:30 a.m. until 2:30 p.m.. We were on what in Chicago is called closed campus. This means that the students come to school at 9:00 a.m. and leave at 2:30 p.m. It includes a 20-minute lunch and, unfortunately, no recess. Ostensibly, Chicago schools started began turning to the closed campus option to prevent problems when the students left the campuses and went home for lunch. Sometimes there were fights. Sometimes they just never came back.

We teachers, too, only had twenty minutes for lunch on this closed campus schedule. We also had preparation periods, while students went to art or library or PE. Unless you made a concerted effort to go down to the teacher's lounge during those short breaks, it was possible that you would never have a serious or extended conversation with another adult in your entire workday. The isolation of the individual teacher was still the rule rather than the exception. You were on your own.

The other thing that I noticed quickly about the staff was the attitude of defeat on the part of the teachers at Marquette. It turned out that their Quest proposal for small schools had been a sham. The teachers hadn't wanted "small schools." The principal had. The principal, it seems, decided that Marquette would have four small schools. He decided what their emphases would be. He picked the teachers who would become the "lead teachers," teachers freed up from classroom responsibilities to oversee each small school's implementation. Voila! Marquette had small schools.

Not so fast. Small schools were being imposed on the staff, but that didn't mean the staff had to like them, or support them.

Teachers also were extremely concerned about the lack of preparedness and the lack of progress of their students. Far too often, I heard negative comments about the students, as if they had any say over their wretched conditions. I began to realize that the teacher' sense of defeat was due primarily to a feeling that nothing was ever going to change.

I remember my first Marquette PPAC (Professional Personnel Advisory Committee) meeting. (This was the legislatively created body, elected by teachers, to give advice on curriculum matters to the principal and the LSC). It was called one morning in September, about my third week at Marquette. The purpose of the meeting was to pick a new chairperson, because the person who had been chairing the PPAC was moving on. There was only one problem. No one would volunteer to be PPAC chair. No one. The outgoing chair cajoled, almost pleaded. Still, no one volunteered.

After many minutes of painful silence, I found myself raising my hand.

"I didn't like the 1988 Chicago school reform law," I began. "I didn't think that giving teachers only two seats on the LSC was fair." I looked around cautiously, watching my new colleagues, wondering what they were thinking.

"We all know how much our 'advice' has traditionally been valued in schools. But the PPAC is all we've got, so it's better than nothing."

I looked around. They were listening intently.

"I know I'm the new kid on the block here," I continued. "But if no one else wants to take this chair, and if my being new isn't a problem for all of you, I'll do it."

I was elected unanimously. Surprise, surprise.

In the weeks that followed, the naysayers told me that nothing would change anyway as a result of our efforts, while I insisted that they could. I said that we at least had to try to change the things we didn't like. At least we could put our issues and concerns in writing to the principal and the LSC, be on record as taking a stand. That would be something. What was the alternative? By law, the LSC had at least to listen to us, right?

So we planned to meet biweekly. We came in early so that we could have an hour of uninterrupted time. We met and we planned, and we assessed the staff's needs and concerns. The continuing, major concern of the faculty was over the lack of academic progress of so many of our kids. Many teachers realized that the "whole language" reading series that they had purchased in 1992 was a problem While it consisted of a beautiful anthology of children's literature, by now it was apparent that it lacked the structure and the systematic attention to phonics skills, which our students so desperately needed. As a group we decided that we would start by looking for a reading series or program that could better serve our student population. It was time to revise our reading series anyway, so we wanted to make the best possible decision about what to use.

Our PPAC included elected representatives of each grade level in the school. These members had a vote. Any faculty member, could attend the PPAC meetings and hear what was being discussed and weigh in with his or her opinion. We had surprisingly good attendance at our meetings. Teachers were beginning to break down the isolation a little bit, to see what others were saying and thinking.

On the reading series issue, we spent over six months previewing and reviewing every possible reading series and hearing from publisher' representatives. We discussed and debated the merits and demerits of each series. We finally achieved a consensus on a particular program, an update of our current series. This one had greater attention to phonics and systematic skills instruction. We also were proud of finding a solution that included our bilingual department, which was using a completely different and ancient set of readers. This new edition of our reading program had a match in readers and materials in Spanish, too.

So we dutifully forwarded our recommendation for a new reading series and a host of other recommendations to our principal and the

Local School Council. The additional recommendations had been culled from regular PPAC meetings, from grade level meetings, and from a needs assessment of the entire staff. Our report included our recommendation, for example, that our school remain a K-5 grade school. (Our new addition was in its final stages and the principal wanted to expand to grades K-8.) We also recommended reducing class sizes in our first grades. While we were pleased at what we had accomplished, I was becoming concerned about the next step. How would the LSC respond?

As PPAC chair, I was attending the Marquette LSC meetings, ostensibly to report on the work of the PPAC. I was astonished to find these meetings farcical. Rarely was there a quorum. When there was, the sessions were nothing but shouting matches between the principal and one of the two elected teacher reps, also our CTU delegate. The two of them had a history of conflict, and their antagonisms became the heart of the LSC meetings for at least the year that I attended them. Little business was accomplished, as far as I could see. Many fights were over the vacant LSC positions and whether someone the principal wanted, or someone Rudy wanted, would prevail. It was depressing. Usually it was the principal's choice who ended up in the vacant position and so, with many allies on the LSC, the principal usually had his way on everything. The meetings were held during school time also. Most staff members could not attend.

We never received the new reading series. We had left in June that year believing that we'd have the new series for our students in September. September came, but the books never did. Something else had come up over the summer, and the principal decided to use the money for that instead. Our school went K-8 and the class sizes in our first grades remained unchanged. So much for our input. So much for us. So much for our students.

That September, when we had the first PPAC meeting of the year to elect a chair, I recommended that we disband the PPAC. After chairing the PPAC for two years, I realized that the naysayers were right: Given the current power structure with the principals having total discretion in decision making and teachers having "input," we weren't going to get anywhere.

"This is not a fight to be waged at the school level," I said to my colleagues after recommending disbanding our PPAC. By this time, I was the CTU delegate, also.

"It's an issue of power at the system level," I continued. "As we all know too well, we have no formal, institutionalized base of power. The principal doesn't have to listen to us. He is simply using the power that he has to ignore our input."

I looked around. They were with me.

"No," I continued, "the fight is at the system level, and I blame the current CTU leadership for the situation in which we are. We must have a union leadership that will fight for our right to have a say in our schools. That is why I believe that we have to work to change our union leadership."

The faculty voted unanimously to disband our PPAC.

It was three months before our principal found out that he didn't have a PPAC anymore. Doesn't that say something about how much teacher input is thought of and valued? Meanwhile, due to the staff's passive aggression, the principal's small schools "movement" died a slow and quiet death. When the people involved in the change effort do not have any ownership of the proposed change, they will not support it. It's a simple as that. They may be afraid of speaking up against the change. They may look like they are changing. But they are not really wholeheartedly carrying out the change because it wasn't their change, but change imposed on them.

Marquette teachers feared reprisals if they spoke against something that the principal wanted. They had seen too many of their outspoken colleagues being sent to the branch school, Marquette's version of Siberia. The Branch was a place where the working conditions were not as good as in the main building. our former CTU representative was a lifer at the branch.

Marquette's principal was not a tyrant. He was a rather pleasant man who wanted people to like him and to believe that he had the students at heart. Most of the time he is and he does. But do not cross him. Do not disagree with him. Do not question him. I have received many apologies from him for blowing up at me in my capacity as CTU delegate, some actually in writing. There is a kind of quid pro quo at the school. He won't bother you if he thinks you are doing your job and you don't question his decisions. Most staff members go along with it. But at a price. The price is their professional self esteem and their belief that anything will ever change.

But things did change at Marquette. And it was the teachers who made the change. I don't think anyone was more surprised than the teachers themselves at just how big a change it was.

As the CTU delegate, I held monthly meetings for union members. I also chaired the PPC (Professional Problems Committee) which, by contract, met monthly with the principal to discuss contractual issues. (For contrast, the PPAC was a legislatively created body to advise the principal and the LSC about curriculum matters). At union meetings and at our staff development meetings, I continued to advocate that teachers take the lead on school improvement at Marquette.

"Do we want to get to the point of being put on probation and having someone else's program forced on us? Or do we want to be pro active and find a way ourselves to improve the achievement of our students?" I would ask. I realized the contradiction of disbanding our PPAC and advocating teacher leadership for change. I still believed that some change was possible. We just had to figure out what it was and then work around the system to do it, if we had to.

One initiative I thought might help came from a program the AFT had written about called "reciprocal teaching." They described it as a process of teaching reading that produced substantial gains in reading comprehension. The model had been developed jointly between the

University of Illinois at Champaign-Urbana and the Springfield, Illinois Public School System. I liked that already, the idea of a research base, and of teachers and researchers working collaboratively on real world issues and applications.

The basic idea underlying this model was to teach struggling readers the strategies that expert readers used automatically in their reading. With such explicit skill and strategy instruction, poor readers were made aware of these things that expert readers did when they read; then they could consciously begin to use them, too, to increase their understanding and retention of what they read.

I had heard speakers discuss the model at the Quest Center conferences. It sounded promising, and we had begun to train teachers in the reciprocal teaching process. I did a few sessions on reciprocal teaching for my Marquette colleagues at some of our staff development sessions. Several teachers expressed an interest in exploring the model further. Reciprocal teaching is intensive, that is, it requires much teacher support, talk and feedback. This is difficult in schools with large class sizes. Researchers found a way to deal with large class sizes, and still have an effect. It was to train student leaders in each classroom to lead reciprocal teaching-like discussions in groups of four and five students. I offered to train up to five student leaders for any teacher who thought he or she might want to try it in the classroom. Much to my surprise over 20 teachers requested the training for their classrooms.

It took me eight weeks—during my daily preparation periods—to train 100 student leaders. The kids were identified as good readers and seen as leaders among their peers. It was a wonderful eight weeks. I worked with Marquette's best and brightest students, and they were wonderful children, eager and excited to be selected as student leaders. Sometimes working in special education, and in hearing all of the negative comments about poor student achievement, you can forget that there are such talented and motivated students in your school. My experience training them as student leaders was probably more rewarding for me than for them.

Teachers in most of those 20 classrooms began reciprocal teaching. Things were going well, according to the teachers involved. They would come up to me in the hallway and tell me great stories about what was happening in their classrooms. I only wished there had been more time to provide follow-up and ongoing support for the student leaders as well as the teachers. There was only so much time in the day, and I had my regular assignment to tend to. Over time, without feedback and follow-up, and hampered by class changes each year, reciprocal teaching faded out. But it was the beginning, in a way, of something momentous that the Marquette faculty accomplished, something that surprised us all.

Along with the 1995 reform law which gave control of the schools to the mayor came an almost hysterical emphasis on student test scores. The mayor was now going to be held accountable; he had to prove that the city's schools were turning around. Underperforming schools were being placed on probation with mandates to bring test scores up. Threats of reconstituting low performing schools were in the air. There was tremendous pressure on principals to show gains in student achievement.

One morning the principal asked me to stop in and see him. Curious, I went to his office and was surprised by his question.

"Would you be interested in doing something different next year? he asked me. "Now I know that you are running for union office, and believe me, I hope that you win," he said with a smile. "But just in case, I was thinking that we need someone to help the teachers work on improving our students' reading skills and also to do something with our half days for staff development."

Though I said I'd think about it, my first thought was to reject a position that would take me out of the classroom to become some kind of "lead" teacher that no one wanted doing something else to the faculty that no one asked for. We had too many freed up people already—two curriculum coordinators, a bilingual lead teacher, an "activities" coordinator, two assistant principals. Because they did not teach, our class sizes were higher and many staff members resented them. This offer seemed like the kiss of death to me.

Then I remembered a program I had been reading about over the past few years out of Johns Hopkins University. It was called *Success For All*. It was one of the reform models that the AFT was encouraging locals to look at as they got involved in school reform issues. Success For All, or SFA, had been created by researchers Robert Slavin and Nancy Madden and had evolved from their earlier work on cooperative learning. I called and requested information.

When I read through what SFA had sent me, I became excited. Here was a research-based program with proven success in helping urban schools with high proportions of students at risk of reading failure: Success For All is a comprehensive approach to restructuring elementary schools to ensure the success of every child. The program emphasizes prevention and early intervention to anticipate and solve any learning problems. Success for All provides schools with research-based curriculum materials; extensive professional development in proven strategies for instruction, assessment and classroom management; one-to-one tutoring for primary grade children who need it; and active family support approaches.

I especially liked the commitment to success for all, to the idea that we cannot stop short of anything less. By targeting prevention and early intervention, SFA research found that first graders who remained in SFA classes were at or above grade level by third grade. Research showed the most improvement, in fact, with the lowest quarter of the school population.

I also liked the fact that Success for All didn't just take anyone into its reform network. In fact, knowing that change imposed on people doesn't work, the SFA office insists on a faculty vote to adopt SFA; 80 percent of the faculty must vote for the program to qualify to become an SFA school. Otherwise, forget it. SFA leaders understand the hard work of change, and they insist on program ownership of those involved in the change. The program also requires that a teacher, not an administrator, be freed full time from classroom duties to help the carrying out of the SFA model.

Since I was reluctant to take on something the faculty didn't want, the hurdle of an 80 percent vote would gauge my decision. If enough of the faculty voted to become an SFA school, then it would be their program, and they would own it. Then I would feel comfortable being their facilitator.

The next step was to invite someone from SFA out to provide an overview of the program to our staff. We listened. We read articles and research. We sent a team of teachers to observe another school in Chicago that was an SFA school to see what it was all about. A presentation was made to our LSC with the principal's strong suggestion that they support his recommendation to include SFA in the budget for the next year. It would be a three-year commitment and would cost $76,000 in the first year, $34,000 in the second, and $24,000 in the third. Then we voted.

Our first vote was 50 Yes and 19 No. By this time, I was so interested and hopeful that I couldn't imagine the proposal not getting enough votes. After we counted the ballots, I walked around the school feeling disappointed and especially sorry for the students. Some teachers came to me and asked for more time and another vote. Perhaps more information, they suggested. Perhaps another group on a site visit, they thought.

"We really need this program in our school," they said, pleading with me to figure out a way to redo things.

We did do those things that they asked. Another team did go. More articles were copied and shared. Questions and answers were sent back and forth between Marquette and SFA headquarters at Johns Hopkins. The second vote had the same result. Nothing had changed.

I was angry now. All the groaning and moaning about how things will never change, and here were 19 of my colleagues voting against change! They had no one to blame but themselves if nothing ever changes, I thought. How could 19 people who don't want to do something keep the 50 of us who do from trying something that we believed would benefit our students? It just didn't seem fair, though I also agreed completely with SFA that if you didn't have 80 percent, you didn't have a good chance at implementation and commitment.

Then it occurred to me. Maybe those 19 didn't have to keep the rest of us from making progress! Marquette's new building addition was now up and running. It was essentially another school laid right along side the original one, two completely separate buildings. Each had at least two sections of every grade, each had its own complement of art, music, gym and library teachers. The only thing the two buildings really shared was the same kitchen. There were even two sets of lunchrooms. What if we went back to Johns Hopkins and guaranteed them 100 percent commitment and SFA operating in one of our two buildings? With more than 2,000 students at Marquette, half of them formed a school larger than most other schools where SFA could be found anyway?

We had to wait weeks for the answer from Johns Hopkins, but it was worth our patience. Though they were reluctant, they could see our point. One half of Marquette is a big school. One hundred percent commitment was enticing. Perhaps, if it flew, our other building would buy into it eventually, too. They gave us a go-ahead.

Then the hard work of change really began. I have never worked so hard in my life. John Kotsakis' phrase "Real change is real hard" was never so true as it was in our first year as an SFA school.

SFA had a mandatory week-long training session for a new SFA school for principals and facilitators. The week provided an overview of the model, and I came away even more impressed. At the AFT, I had been involved with several different education reform groups: the Coalition of Essential Schools, the Small Schools Movement, the schools trying Hoard Garner's Theories of Multiple Intelligences, and several more. I had never seen a reform model so thorough, so systematic and so rich. I felt like I had died and gone to heaven.

A 90-minute block of time for reading lies at the heart of the program. For the reading program, students are grouped according to their reading ability. You use staff completely differently in an SFA school. Every certified person in the building possible takes a reading group. In our case, all of our LD resource teachers and our additional remedial teachers from Chapter 1 funds took a reading class. This changed our class size from an average of 34 to an average of 20 for ninety minutes every day! Now you are talking about significant, structural changes.

Then what went into those ninety minutes was state-of-the-art teaching practice in reading and writing, particularly for children at high risk of reading failure. We assess and regroup children every eight weeks, as necessary to move them along as fast as possible. You also commit to tutoring 30 percent of your lowest first graders and 20 percent of your lowest second graders. Prevention and early intervention. This tutoring, unlike most, is also state-of-the-art, intensive, and totally tied to exactly what was taught that morning in the reading class.

There is a strong family support component, in line with the SFA commitment not to let any child fall through the cracks. Teachers refer students to the Family Support Team when they have additional problems which prevent them from learning. This could be chronic truancy or tardiness, suspected abuse or neglect, or severe behavior problems. The team works with the home to identify all of the possible resources of the family, school and community to bring to bear on the child's academic situation.

Ninety minutes for reading might appear to be a large amount of time. Yet the problem most SFA teachers face, especially in the first year, is getting everything accomplished in that frame; the program is that rich. Another feature of the program that I felt was critical were implementation visits from the SFA staff. You make a three year commitment to SFA. In the first year there are three implementation visits by John Hopkins staff to provide feedback on how well you are doing carrying out the model. This is important to help maintain fidelity to the program.

There is a natural ebb and flow in the change process. People initially are excited about any change, but then can get discouraged at the hard work of change or the lack of instant results when you are trying so hard. It is important to get feedback on how well you are doing. You also need to hear that the issues and concerns you have about yourselves and your students are to be expected in first year schools.

Another important element in SFA implementation is the role of the facilitator. SFA is designed to draw on teacher leadership, another reason that it has become near and dear to my heart. At one SFA conference I heard Robert Slavin say, "We now know that public school teachers can change what is wrong with public schools if they are given the right tools to do so." Yes, we can. Yes, we can!

At the new sites training, I wondered why the trainers would playfully bow down to the new facilitators, but now I know. Being a facilitator, especially in a first year SFA school, is difficult at a stunning level. The facilitator coordinates everything about the program, from the tremendous number of materials provided (you don't have to get a new reading series because they have coordinated all of their materials to current series); assigning of the children to groups and then assessing and regrouping them every eight weeks; providing support and peer coaching to all of the SFA teachers (which means observation and feedback to help them strengthen their implementation of the program); coordinating the tutoring of all of the children who require it and providing support to the tutors; substituting in SFA reading classes when there are no trained subs (which is a constant problem); participating on the Family Support Team; coordinating all professional development activities; communicating and reporting to SFA staff, and much, much more.

The spring before we began Success for All, the principal decided that he wanted to create a wing of the school as the Enrichment wing.

He unilaterally took the 30 top scoring students in every grade, creamed the student body in other words, and began the Marquette Enrichment program. SFA and all of the other classes were now at a huge disadvantage now without our best and brightest (in both academics and behavior). The faculty didn't want this and let Fred know it, but several of our LSC members' children ended up in the Enrichment wing and so we knew we wouldn't get anywhere trying to fight it.

Despite this disadvantage, the teachers pressed on. Most were overwhelmed the first year. For many, the approach is different from what they learned in teacher education programs. A tremendous amount of cooperative learning is incorporated in the program. Cooperative learning involves children working in teams to learn the material and to help each other learn the material. You have to have excellent classroom and behavior management skills for cooperative learning to work, because kids working together make a lot of noise!

Nor were our students used to working together to solve problems. Many had trouble getting along with each other. Being such an overcrowded school and having students so far behind academically, we had more than our share of behavior problems in our classrooms. That's a challenge for the best of teachers.

SFA requires a fast pace, lots of debate and discussion of materials with the students, and continuing of student writing in response to what they've read. There is a structure to the way vocabulary and new stories are introduced. There are a daily sequence and a weekly sequence. The first twenty minutes of the reading class, for example, are devoted to listening comprehension. Here, teachers read rich literature to their students and ask important questions about what is read and the author's craft in writing it. Even the older children loved to be read to and challenged with provocative questions and discussion. Some teachers liked the structure. Others didn't. Nevertheless, all of them had agreed to set aside the "tried and true" and give SFA a chance.

Our teachers weren't used to working together, either. Now we had a common bond, a common mission to work together to carry out SFA. Our two monthly half-days for professional development became filled with discussion of implementation issues over pot luck lunches where everyone shares a dish. "How do you do this?" "Here is how I handle that." "How can we do this better?" We were learning and growing together. We weren't isolated anymore.

Though it is recommended that the facilitator not have a reading group because of all of the responsibilities of overall implementation, I ended up teaching a group anyway. It was one of the best things that I did all year. Technically, SFA only went through sixth grade, but they had materials designed for sixth and seventh grade novels. Our seventh and eighth grade teachers were so interested in the model that they decided to carry out the program for their students using these novels and other materials. They still had class sizes of 33-35. Their teachers came to me and asked what could be done, especially for their students reading at fourth and fifth grade reading levels. I ended up forming a group comprising the five lowest readers in each of the two seventh and eighth grades, for a total of 20 students and teaching it myself.

Knowing how low in reading these children (most of them taller than I) were, I felt somewhat apprehensive. But I also felt excited about having my own group and having the chance to "do" the model myself. I felt that the experience would add to my ability (and my credibility) to support my colleagues in their efforts to implement the model. I loved it. I loved it. They weren't perfect angels. (Several got suspended several times during the year. Several had probation officers). Yet they were fun, energetic, and painfully aware of their shortcomings. Half of them were eighth graders who wouldn't make it to high school unless they attained a 7.4 reading grade on our standardized tests. Some were extremely motivated and some didn't get motivated until March of the year, losing a lot, for some too much, time.

I learned a lot from them, too, especially about their views on school. One writing assignment my students did for their home room teacher, which she shared with me, was heartbreaking. The students had to do an autobiography. Two essays were particularly haunting. One boy, a tough, "I don't have to do a thing you say" kid wrote, "I loved kindergarten. We had so much fun. I wish I never had to leave my kindergarten class." Another boy described what he wanted to be when he grew up. "I would like to be a wrestling champion and have everyone look at me and see how good I was. I've never been recognized for anything before."

It made me sad to think that we hadn't had a program like SFA in time for these children to make a real difference. Their view of themselves as failures was pretty set. To me SFA was a happy medium between social promotion and holding kids back. Certainly there could be benchmarks for the intermediate, upper grades and high school. SFA provided each child 90 minutes of rich instruction *at their level.* As quickly as possible we taught them, assessed them and moved them. This way they could move on with their age group but be assured of appropriate reading instruction. The way things were now, the upper grade teachers had to *read the textbooks aloud* as more and more of their classes became further and further behind level.

Things weren't perfect at Marquette that first year of starting SFA. We struggled with implementation issues and with concerns over whether SFA would truly benefit our students. We were terribly overcrowded and had SFA reading classes doubled up in classrooms, hallways and even in both lunchrooms. There were concerns about the servicing of our special education children, who are all in SFA reading classes. There were a few teachers who still weren't sure they *liked* the program. Tutors tutored in every nook and cranny of the building. The teachers in the other building complained about the haves and the have-nots, even though they had been the ones that voted *not.*

The principal was not involved in SFA, even though administrative support is crucial to solid implementation of the program. He did pay the bills, though, which was important. I'm not sure he realized or appreciated just how valiantly his SFA staff was working to provide a better education for Marquette students. I knew he would love the program if our test scores went up, though SFA warns that it takes a good three years for the program to show its true effect. The assistant principal in our SFA building was deeply committed, and I could usually count on him to modify or change administrative decisions that negatively affected on the program.

Still, without any real power over school level decision-making, we were at the mercy of the administration whether the program would continue or not. The Chicago SFA school that our team went to observe before starting SFA, for example, was not given that chance. A new principal arrived. She announced she had a Master's degree in reading. She could design a better reading program than Johns Hopkins University could, she informed them. So she abolished SFA at that school, in the middle of their three-year contract. This was a travesty both for the teachers who had invested almost two years in the program and for the students who were left drifting. Rather than stay and fight, which is difficult if you have no formal power or authority, distressed teachers chose to leave. They left in droves.

Meanwhile, I was so proud of us at Marquette. We took a chance and made an important change that we thought was in the best interests of our students and ourselves. Despite the system, we brought our own class sizes down to 20, at least for a substantial part of the day. Yes, we had the agreement of the principal and the LSC and the funds, all of which were critical. Yet we were the ones who put our hearts and souls into trying something new. Taking a risk is scary. Moving from the tried and true to the new is challenging. Charting a course on uncharted waters is frightening, and exciting.

We were doing it. Slavin was absolutely right: public school teachers can fix what is wrong with urban education if given the right tools. But the tool kit is not complete without the power and authority to make decisions about their use. It is not enough to have tools if someone else tells you what to do with them, when to do it and how to do it, or whether you can use them at all. This is how the power structure remains in most schools. Not much had changed since I did my study of professional power and powerlessness. We were making our changes despite the system. Think about the kind of schools and the kind of system we could have if teaching professionals were investing in change and improvement because of the system.

At the end of our first year the results were promising. Even though it takes three years to feel the full impact, our SFA students in grades three through eight achieved 11 percent more than the comparable students in our other building. Even more encouraging, *three times* the number of our first and second graders (or 33 percent) successfully made it to the fourth quarter of the reading program. Only 11 percent had the year before. We were elated at the promise of these numbers for our students.

My own reading class fared pretty well, also. Fifteen of my twenty very-below-level seventh and eighth graders averaged *two years* of growth in reading. For many of them, it made the difference between staying in elementary school or moving on to high school. For me, the experience was rewarding and gave me confidence in my role as the facilitator to support my colleagues.

The beat goes on at Marquette, but no question about it. It was time to try to change the system.

Chapter VIII.
The PACT Years, 1995-1996:
Starting a Movement

When I left the Chicago Teachers Union Quest Center with the thought of running for union office, I had no idea what to expect. That was probably a good thing. Were there people out there who felt as I did about the need for real leadership in our union? Were there enough members dissatisfied with the way things were to take a chance on change? Could someone with a handful of contacts and no war chest mount an effective campaign against incumbents? Incumbents who controlled all the power and conventional tools of the union, the newspaper, the membership lists, and everything else? I was about to find out.

I began reaching out to the many people I had come to know through my work at the Quest Center. After 15 years out of the classroom, they were the CTU members who knew me best and, presumably, these were the members who wanted change in their schools. They had resonated to our call at the Quest Center. Obviously they supported the notion that the union should take the initiative on school reform. What about union reform, I wondered?

In October of 1995, I invited about 50 of those teachers to a dinner at a downtown restaurant to discuss my candidacy. Thirty of them came. I explained my reasons for leaving the union staff and returning to teaching. I said that any campaign couldn't be a "me." It had to be a "we."

"Would you like to have the public view you and your union as part of the solution for education, not part of the problem?" I asked them. "Would you like to see your union leaders aggressively making our case, telling our story to the public and to the legislature? Would you like to see dynamic, visible and pro active union leadership promoting an agenda to give us more say over what we do and what we need to best do our jobs?"

I invited them to join me on a new quest, a quest for the kind of union leadership that the membership deserved. They had seen, probably more than most members, the change at CTU headquarters after Jacqui's death. They had experienced the silence. The lack of new ideas or programs. The lukewarm support of their own school reform efforts from new leaders who didn't think the union had any business in school reform. Fifteen of the thirty teachers attending that dinner signed right up for a campaign committee. We ended up calling our new party PACT, for ProActive Chicago Teachers. Now it was time to go out and find 15 more teachers, and then 15 more teachers after that.

In early November with the help of Laurie Glen we announced our campaign. Laurie was the head of L.R.Glenn Communications, the public relations firm John and I had used sometimes to promote Quest center activities. When she worked with us at the union, Laurie saw right away the apathy and animosity that the CTU communications department had for us and what we were about. She thought that what John and I were doing with the Quest Center could have been a real public relations vehicle for the union. The CTU leadership could have used it to position itself and its members in a positive way in the public's eye. Imagine, a union wanting to do something to improve the schools. She couldn't believe that the Reece team could squander such an opportunity.

When I told Laurie that I was leaving the CTU to run for union office, she volunteered to do the campaign public relations gratis. We quickly developed materials to contrast the incumbent and ourselves. Our first campaign piece provided this contrast:

	Tom Reece & UPC	Debbie Lynch Walsh & PACT
Leadership	Reactive, defensive, rudderless, anonymous	Proactive, comprehensive, visible
Contract	Gutted on his watch	Will fight to restore rights
Salaries	Double dips; collects $175,000+ for two jobs	One job to represent members
Dues	One of nation's highest dues structures	Will trim excess funds to better serve
School decision Making	No position—accepts the status quo LSC	Will lobby for five teacher seats
Privatization	No strategy	Prove union members can do it better
School Intervention	No say in how millions are spent	Press for equal say in expenditures
School Improvement	Views this as management's job	Position the union as part of the solution
State Funding	Fighting to maintain ground	Leverage public confidence to gain ground
Public Outreach	In-house damage control	Outreach & dialogue on issues & CTU positions

These issues responded to many changes that the Illinois legislature had enacted in the spring of 1995. Besides giving the mayor total control of the public schools, it stripped one, just one teachers' union in Chicago of many time-honored union rights. Not other unions across Illinois, just the CTU. In that legislation, CTU members lost the right to bargain class size, layoff procedures, seniority protections, teacher evaluations and more. Teacher assistants and other kinds of paraprofessionals, who comprised about 20 percent of the union membership, became employees at will with no union protections afforded any more at all. Principals now had the power to hire outsiders, employees from private firms, for any job, including teaching jobs.

"It is incredible to note," wrote Tom Reece in a letter to CTU delegates about the legislation, "that an eighteen-month prohibition on our right to strike pales in comparison to the other onerous sections of this legislation."

Even *more* incredibly, Reece went on in the same letter *to blame these terrible losses on CTU members themselves,* not his own highly paid state and local union lobbyists or his leadership team.

"As we have found out in recent elections, too many of our own members do not vote, do not vote for CTU endorsed candidates or encourage their friends and family members to vote for CTU endorsed candidates…And now we see that fewer than 15 percent of our 31,000 members bothered to make the effort of sending a fax to Springfield to save their rights and job protections."

Instead of asking themselves what they could have done to stave off this onerous legislation lobbying in Springfield, or what they could have done to mobilize the membership on these issues, they blamed the membership for it. The CTU members that they had kept in the dark about the legislation, the CTU members that they wanted to keep uninformed, and therefore unquestioning. These same CTU members were now, by some convoluted logic, the source of these devastating losses of our bargaining rights.

Yet two months later, Reece and his team recommended that these members vote for a four-year contract, a contract Reece trumpeted was "made in heaven." Reece claimed that because the new Board of Education was putting the class size limits and teacher discipline issues into board policy, it didn't make any difference that we had lost them contractually. He failed to warn his members that board policy could be changed unilaterally at any time and that the once-powerful CTU could do nothing about such changes. There was another problem with the strategy. When the CTU went to court to try to get these bargaining rigsht back, the judge threw the case out because Reece had signed a deal. "How can you claim that loss of these rights make it impossible for you to bargain, when, in fact, you have done exactly that?" the judge asked, dismissing Reece's argument.

They took a vote on the new contract over the summer, when fewer members were around or tuned into the dubious deal agreed to by the union and the board. A four-year contract with yearly 3 percent raises sounded good. The public was delighted at the thought of four years of labor peace. It wasn't a perfect time to begin a campaign against the CTU incumbents, but we forged ahead.

That November, after much lavish praise and attention from the Reece team, the Board CEO Paul Vallas moved to use some of the many powers the legislature gave him. He instituted an employee discipline code that allowed principals to suspend teachers for up to 15 days without due process.

There was no outcry from the CTU leadership. But that was just the beginning.

I wrote the following letter and circulated it to as many teachers as I could:

"Dear Colleague,

By now you might have heard that I have returned to the classroom and am organizing a campaign to challenge the current CTU officers in next spring's union elections. After trying to work with the present union administration as CTU Quest Center Director, I have come to the conclusion that our present officers simply do not see the danger we are in.

"Throughout last spring's legislative session and even now in the discussions shaping the future of the Chicago Public Schools, these officers have been deafeningly silent. They have no agenda. They are against everything and for nothing. They are perpetuating the stereotype that the union (and its members) are part of the problem, not part of the solution. As a result, the legislature took aim and gutted our contract...and we lost these things on their watch. The Board is also using our pension money, something Reece promised our delegates it wouldn't do when we voted to ratify our recent contract.

"The current officers think that they have solved the problem of our contractual losses because the Board has put many of these things into policy. However, policy is not contract language. We are totally at the

mercy of the Board's unilateral decision making on these issues. We are, in fact, worse off now from a union point of view, than we were before we ever had a collective bargaining law. The results of that legislation and changes in our contract can be seen in the new Employee Discipline Policy, which enables a supervisor to suspend an employee without a hearing. Did the union fight this? Did they mobilize the membership? No, they raised a feeble objection that some principals might abuse the policy and totally missed the point. Our due process rights have been violated and this union leadership can't do anything about it.

"It is time for real leadership to return to the CTU. It is time to remind ourselves about the kind of leadership Jacqueline B. Vaughn provided our union. While we didn't get everything we wanted under Jacqui, we had an activist leader who made our case to the legislature, to the public and to anyone else who would listen. Our present leadership is invisible. Who is speaking for us now?...

"I could not in good conscience remain working for a group of people who I believe are taking us down the wrong road. We are in real danger. Efforts to privatize, voucherize and charterize are being passed in state after state. They are striking closer and closer to home. Many custodial positions in Chicago schools have already been privatized. There is talk that the new schools in each region for dropouts and disruptive children will be contracted out to private groups. CTU members will be next if we cannot make the case that we can do the job better than any privateers can.

"The union is us. It won't change by itself. We have to work to change it. CTU members deserve better. Those who do nothing are supporting the present road to disaster. It is time for a change in our union leadership, time for a new vision, new voice and new visibility in our union at all levels...Join me and fellow CTU members from across the city in developing an agenda that will both protect our jobs and enable us to provide the education that the children we serve deserve."

The Reece team struck back. They took our UPC/PACT comparison and contrast and came up with their own version of it. We were defining the campaign agenda. Here is what they wrote:

UPC: The Real Issues

	Tom Reece & UPC	Debbie Walsh & PACT(?)
Leadership	Strong leadership; proven results	Taught less than five years; never held CTU office
Contract	Overcame legislation: four year contract	No experience fighting for members' rights
Salaries	Same as others had, works 7 days a week	Took full salary while being absent much of the time
Dues	Same as last CTU president	Lack of knowledge of how dues are spent
School Decision Making	Years of experience with school decision making	No practical or lobbying experience
Privatization	Halted attempts to privatize	Publicly stated schools don't need more money
School improvement	involved staff in community outreach	Not familiar w/CTU staff's role
Public outreach	Successful in changing media perception	Paid Quest specialist now serves her for free

While I had expected personal attacks, I still was shocked at the hits about my "absenteeism." The statement "Took full salary while being absent much of the time" was an attack on the flex time arrangement that I had arranged with Jacqui Vaughn. I hadn't been absent. I had been working at home on certain days and at certain times, as we had agreed. I remembered how complicated it was being a single mom, getting three small children and myself up and going in the morning. Those three ten-hour days began with a taxi picking the four of us up, dropping my first grader off at her school, then my two preschool tykes off at their preschool, and finally, me, breathless, at the train station, all by 7:45

a.m.. It had been worth it to me, however, because I had loved every minute of working at the Quest Center. That attack was truly unfair.

The whisper campaign was even more vicious. People were told that I had just had too many personal family tragedies and had gone over the deep end. In a way this viciousness told me volumes about the incumbent' fear of my candidacy, of our PACT.

Despite the attacks—the public ones and the whisper campaigns—slowly but surely our little committee grew. Our data base grew. Thanks to Laurie, we obtained some decent press. Word was getting out. We were not the first group to try to challenge the Reece party, or caucus. His caucus was the UPC (United Progressive Caucus). Reece had been challenged in the 1994 election by long time union opposition leader George Schmidt of TAC (Teachers Action Committee), renamed CDU (Committee for a Democratic Union). Schmidt's group had also challenged Jacqui Vaughn in the late 1980's and surprised everyone by getting 42 percent of the vote. CDU obtained 28 percent in 1994 in the election that occurred shortly after Jacqui's death. CDU was particularly strong in the high schools, where much of the dissatisfaction with the CTU leadership existed.

Schmidt had a strong and tough reputation made many elementary school teachers uneasy. I called him before I announced to see if he, too, was thinking of challenging Reece. This time around, he had other things on his plate. Though some CDU members gave advice, money and moral support to the PACT campaign, we all thought that distancing PACT from TAC and CDU was a good thing. This was a new challenge and we wanted to emphasize that fact.

PACT was large enough to slate members for just about all of the available positions, which was quite a few. In addition to the local election for five officers and about 40 executive board members, the delegates to the state and national union conventions were also elected. We had to slate 150 delegates and 45 alternates for those positions, also. Overall, our total slate was impressive. We had teachers and paraprofessionals from schools throughout the city, of all races and at all levels, high school and elementary.

The next hurdle was garnering more than 2,000 signatures on our petitions to qualify to get on the ballot. This is a complicated process whereby only the constituent groups can sign petitions and vote for their constituency's executive board candidates. In other words, only teacher assistants could sign for teacher assistants, and so on. We were unable to get signatures for several paraprofessional categories, such as school clerks and teacher assistants, which hurt us badly, but we simply ran out of time and contacts. Fortunately, we slated, school clerk Barbara Hammonds, as one of our five officer candidates. Slating a paraprofessional in an officer position was a first in the CTU. We hoped that this might cancel out any hard feelings about the executive board spots.

As excited as we were about Barbara's candidacy, we were totally deflated when we were told that she didn't qualify to be on the ballot. We had hoped her candidacy would send a message to those 6,000 paraprofessionals that we were making a statement about just how important they were to the union. Barbara would make sure that their issues were heard and addressed. It turned out that she hadn't been a CTU member for the three years before the election, a key requirement to run for union office. She had worked with the Board of Education for at least six, but the first four in a paraprofessional position that was not represented by the CTU, but another union. It was an embarrassment to have only four out of five officer candidates slated. But we vowed to go forward.

The next big hurdle was trying to get a fair election. I had no idea what we were facing. I was unaware of the mechanics of the CTU elections. Now I would learn more than I ever wanted to know about them.

Lou Pyster was a CTU member and part of the opposition to the UPC for decades. He had been the lone questioning voice on the CTU Rules-Election Committee since the mid-seventies. He had been appointed to this committee several presidents back. He seemed to be the one to ask for information and counsel. When we asked for a briefing, he outlined his many concerns about the election rules and procedures. We were shocked. We wrote to Reece and the CTU Rules Election Committee in January before the May election articulating these concerns.

First, there were no adequate controls over the total number of ballots. The committee consists of 30 members, 29 of whom were UPC incumbent candidates. The committee did not release the number of ballots printed, the number of unused or spoiled ballots or the election report sheets that each school completes with the numbers of voters and unused ballots.

Second, there are too many movements of the ballots without adequate protections. Voting occurs in almost 600 schools. The election judge in each school then either brings the ballots to the CTU office or to one of the three drop-off points around the city. A messenger service collects them and brings them in. This is done so that the canvassing committee can check for discrepancies. They bring in the ballots and out via the office building's loading docks over a period of several hours. They move the ballots out again, taken in multiple van trips to the final destination, a data processing firm, located two hours away, which counts the votes. There is absolutely no way observers can stay with the ballots at all times.

Our third concern was the large period of time that the election and the ballots themselves were in the virtually exclusive control of UPC incumbent candidates. That 30-member Rule-Election Committee which conducts and oversees the election had 29 UPC candidates on it. That meant that election decisions were not in impartial hands. A little like letting the Democrats or Republicans handle the ballots in the City of Chicago Election, rather than the Board of Elections.

Reece referred our letter to the CTU Rules-Election Committee; we were told that there was "no basis for your concerns. The Rules-Election Committee has always been and shall continue to ensure a fair, safe and informed election to our brothers and sisters."

Not satisfied with this response, we appealed to the AFT to look at the CTU election rules. We were told that the AFT Constitution required any such request be approved by the officers or by 30 percent of the local's membership. By now it was February and we didn't have that kind of time. We also sought assistance from the U.S. Department of Labor, but their representatives informed us that they could not intervene until *after* election irregularities occurred. We then tried to take our appeal to the CTU House of Delegates. We wrote to each one and explained why we needed certain changes in the election rules to ensure a fair election.

"The UPC incumbents will try to ensure that they remain in control of the election process unless you take action" we wrote. "The real issues are that we never know how many ballots are printed. The incumbents control the election process…Please join us in insisting on enough safeguards and controls to ensure an honest election, so that CTU members can have confidence in their election process." We lost that battle. The House of Delegates approved rules, and we had to live with them.

The viciousness continued. In a UPC letter, signed by all of the incumbent CTU officers, union members were told that I was waging a battle "designed to weaken our union. Don't let her tactics and dirty tricks deter you from spreading the truth about this election…Our opponent has a dismal record of chronic absence from the office where she formerly worked. She failed to follow through with schools to which she was assigned. She wasn't even a CTU member for years when she could have been!...If you or anyone in your school is asked to sign a PACT petition, we urge you to decline. PACT doesn't represent anyone who has worked in our schools. It represents the positions of one untrustworthy individual who wants to continue using our union for her own personal gain."

In a way, all these attacks from the CTU leaders themselves were helping to put me and our caucus on the map. If we were threat enough for Reece himself to sign such a letter, some members thought, then this group must be a group to be reckoned with. I quickly responded with a statement to all CTU delegates explaining my flex time arrangement with Jacqui Vaughan. I said that while in Washington, I was a member of another union, AFTSU, and so couldn't be in both unions. I questioned the UPC's courage if they were so afraid of a fair contest that they had to scare members into not signing our petitions.

The campaign fight went on. We produced literature challenging their use of our exorbitant dues, the erosion of our contract and our rights, the loss of our union power and professional respect. They kept trying to claim "four years of stability through the four-year contract, while saving our job and seniority protections and holding the board to our class size provisions," statements that were far from true. They also kept up the personal attacks, claiming that I was the "founder and lone voice of PACT...was completely out of touch with union reality...can't begin to understand what unionism was all about." The comparisons were interesting; Reece and his cohort claimed that I was "like that well-known master of deceit and negativism, Pat Buchanan, she is attempting to distort all the good things about our union into things sinister." They even tried to have me thrown off of the ballot because a part of my membership was paid retroactively, but in that they were unsuccessful.

By this time our committee had grown to thirty regulars, teachers and paraprofessionals, who would meet weekly to strategize and stuff envelopes. By May, we had contacts in about 250 of the 580 Chicago schools, members willing to pass out our literature and spread the word. We had to rely on this system because we did not have a membership list nor the funds to do first class mailings to 31,000 union members. In an effort to reach out to as many people as possible, we invested in making a video highlighting our candidates and our issues. My friend Michael Humphries, a professional videographer, gave us a big break on the cost. Even though it was low budget, it turned out well. We then sent one copy to each of our school contacts in the hopes that they would share it widely.

Also during the campaign, we dashed from school to school in the early morning or after school to talk to CTU members. The union delegate or an interested member would ask us to come out, publicize the meeting (sometimes in their homes and even their churches), and provide refreshments. Personally I was able to visit about 50 different schools during the campaign, but it was rough campaigning and working full time. These school visits gave me hope, however, because at every one there were people pulling out their checkbooks and encouraging us to hang in there. At every one there were teachers resonating to the issues we were raising. Many of them had been unaware of the rights we had lost. For many of those who cared enough to come early and stay late to hear about union issues, it was a wake-up call, and I could see that. They would admit that they hadn't really paying attention to what was going on in the union. Many thought everything had been going okay because they had been told to think that.

Then came the election countdown. Tradition dictated that the candidates for president had 10 minutes at the May House of Delegates meeting to speak to the delegates about their candidacies. Here is what I said to the delegates on May 9, 1996, after introducing the other PACT officer candidates:

I will do three things in this speech: tell you who I am, what we think the issues are, and what the PACT team intends to do about them. First, we need a union that will take the lead on important issues, instead of merely reacting to management. We need a union that insists on trust and professional respect for its members, and, through the contract, negotiates an equal say for its members on all of the important decisions affecting their jobs. We need a union that so aggressively and effectively makes the case for its members that they are proud to be union again.

We can have such a union. Would you like to see the CTU strong again? Would you like to be part of winning things back again, to be part of a real "union movement" again? Then join me and PACT. And who am I? I am a mother and a teacher. A democrat and a unionist. I believe in the legacy of the union movement, its rich history and past contributions to society. I also believe in its future and the contribution we can make to the lives of our members and the students we serve.

I am running for CTU president. People run for office all the time. It's the American way. I am exercising the right we all have guaranteed to us in the CTU Constitution, the right to run for union office. I have the nerve to challenge these officers because I believe that they are taking our union down the road to disaster. They are so fearful of a challenge upsetting the good things they have going for themselves that they have stooped to character assassination, harassment and undermining the democratic process in our union. They have tried to harass PACT candidates and intimidate PACT members...No one should be treated with the kind of negativity and contempt that I have seen in this election and the last one. You try to crush your opposition and you eliminate the only source of improving things and changing the direction of the union that you have. Discussion and debate strengthen, not weaken, democracy. This union's power is used more against its internal opponents than against our real adversaries...

Look at what we lost on their watch. They will say that things are fine, that we have a four-year contract and a great relationship with management. Well, if things are so good, why do our members feel so bad, so demoralized, so downtrodden? We'll continue to have a great relationship with management as long as we roll over for them. Our contract, in fact, is not guaranteed. We are at the mercy of the Board's decision as to whether there is enough money to pay for it. This 'contract made in heaven' was the same contract that all of the Board unions got, even the school firemen, whom they permanently displaced and are now gone. But according to Tom Reece, if they are not CTU members, we don't have to worry about them. The only problem is, we may be next. We have no leverage, no allies, no base. This leadership has not done what needs to be done to get the public on our side. And when the public is not on your side, the politicians think they can get away with anything. And they do.

Over the past two years our union has been weakened, our contract gutted, and our hard earned right trampled upon. The once powerful Chicago Teachers Union has become a nonentity. We are vilified, yet marginalized in school politics. Ironically, under this team, we look more and more like a company union every day...

Where were they when Paul Vallas gave his word that he wouldn't touch our pensions and then took $64 million after we ratified the contract? Where were they when they passed the regressive Employee Discipline Code? Where are they now as the Board moves to privatize union jobs—even teaching jobs—in the name of school improvement? Where were they when the Illinois legislature gutted our contract? What are they doing to counter the ever-increasing power of the principals who, in effect, are more beholden to the members of the LSC's than the members of their faculties?

Our caucus is committed to the following five things. We will 1.) Fight to regain all that has been lost to us on their watch...2.) Press for true labor management cooperation and an equal say on key decisions...3.) Fight to counter the new powers of the principal...4.) Work for a more open, more democratic union....5.) Support the delegates in their roles as union leaders...

Would you like to be part of a union where bold ideas and innovative thinking are welcome, not viewed with distrust and suspicion? Where dialogue, discussion and debate are valued, not ridiculed and berated? Where members feel an identification with and a loyalty to their union, not cynicism and apathy? The choice is clear. Cling to the past or take a chance on a better future. Stay with a closed, secret society or choose an open, vital organization; stick with the current passive, defensive, reactive style or vote for a proactive, dynamic agenda.

We, too, can leave a legacy. We can do it if we have the faith and the courage and the vision of a different kind of union: one which promotes a sense of mission and belonging, a sense of empowerment for the delegates and for the members. This is what creates the power of the union. The union is us. It will not change unless we change it. The current officers have forgotten what the lines of Solidarity Forever tell us. "What force on earth is feebler than the feeble strength of one. For the union makes us strong." It's time to take back our union. Thank you.

Much to my amazement, I received a strong round of applause after the speech and several times I was interrupted by applause during the speech. This was amazing because most of the 200 people on the UPC slate were CTU delegates. The House meetings averaged about 500 delegates in attendance. When you considered that two to three hundred of them were UPC candidates or UPC members compared to our handful, the response was respectable. I had hit a nerve.

They held the election Friday, May 17. We were all exhausted but optimistic. We still had our concerns about the fairness of the election process, but that was out of our hands. While the voting occurred that day, we had to wait for four days to find out the vote count. The count was done by a data processing firm, a firm selected and paid for by the incumbents. We were there the following Tuesday and learned that Tom Reece had won with 13,957 votes (or 72.8 percent) to my 5,214 votes (27.2 percent). It was time to call for an investigation of the election.

Looking back now, getting the support of more than 5,000 of my colleagues the first time I ran seems like a big accomplishment. Our slate was relatively unknown in most schools. We hadn't had the time or the resources to combat such a lack of name recognition or to combat the power and the resources of the incumbents. Nevertheless, thousands of people *had* voted for us. It was a start, I thought. If we could hang together for two more years until the next election, which seemed so far away, who knew what we could do next time? Meanwhile, we had an election challenge to mount.

First, we needed to see if we had a case to stand on in challenging the election. I had recently read a great book about unions and union elections called **Which Side Are You On? How to be for Labor When It's Flat on its Back** by Thomas Geoghegan. In it he detailed his work as a labor lawyer fighting big management, and in several cases fighting big labor over lack of internal union democracy. The book jacket said he lived in Chicago, so I called him up and asked him if he would help us. Much to my surprise he and his law partner, renowned former Alderman Leon Despres, agreed to do so. They thought we had a case and assisted me in drafting the challenge itself. The first step was to appeal to the AFT.

Albert Shanker and several of the AFT Executive Council members advocated doing an investigation of our charges. They voted to authorize an investigation. This, although Tom Reece, by virtue of being CTU and IFT (Illinois Federation of Teachers) president, was on both the 38 member AFT Executive Board and the even more powerful five member AFT Executive Committee. We were encouraged. We were sure that after the investigators looked at what occurred in the election, they would surely overturn it and order a new election.

This wasn't the case. President Shanker was gravely ill with cancer and the investigation was turned over to his Secretary-Treasurer. A committee came to Chicago to hear testimony from both sides. Even during the hearing, it became clear to me that we weren't going to get anywhere at this level. Some committee members actually acted hostile to our charges. They weren't concerned that the incumbents ran the election. They weren't concerned that candidates actually handled ballots during the canvassing process. They weren't concerned that the CTU wouldn't release the school election reports or tell us the number of unused ballots.

Not surprisingly, within a month we received the committee's response. They upheld the election. Our challenge had been to *the fairness of the election process and the rules themselves*. The AFT committee rephrased the question and concluded with the answer that it desired. The committee said the issue was "whether there were violations of the CTU Election Rules in the May 1996 elections, and if so, whether such violations are likely to have affected the outcome of the election." *We never charged that there had been rule violations.* The committee concluded, disappointingly, that "in the end, this election should stand. We find no irregularities or violations of the AFT or CTU Constitution."

There was one more avenue of redress. The last step was to appeal to the U.S. Secretary of Labor. The Labor Department, too, launched an investigation of the election—however, only the election of the AFT and IFT delegates. Surprisingly, it does not have jurisdiction over public employee unions. The only way they had standing was due to the fact that the AFT and IFT have private employee unions in their ranks. Therefore they fall under the jurisdiction of the Labor Department and the LMRDA (Labor Management Reporting and Disclosure Act), a federal law that governs union elections.

It took two years for the answer to arrive. The Labor Department, too, let the election stand, but provided a response to each of our concerns. They found that the CTU *had* violated federal election law and *had* violated the CTU Constitution. Yet we could not prove that those violations would have affected the outcome of the election. This is the Labor Department standard. Unless it can be proven, which is nearly impossible if you don't actually witness balloting tampering of thousands of ballots, they can't by law overturn an election. Still, their report was revealing. It found that "all ballots could not be accounted for…3,423 ballots were unaccounted for and presumably destroyed"; that the participation of the major candidates in the canvassing process "did appear to be in violation of the CTU Constitution and By-Laws"; that "about 100 of the six hundred ballot box envelopes had been opened at the canvass, and some ballot box envelopes were not sealed or completely sealed, and some were resealed when they arrived at the canvass."

"In summary," the report continued, "the complainant's allegations of errors in the handling of the ballots were in several instances confirmed. The CTU should improve its handling procedures and adopt and enforce safeguards to assure that all election materials, including unused ballots, are retained in future elections…The investigation failed to disclose violations which may have affected the outcome of the election…Accordingly, we are closing our file on this matter."

The CTU leadership crowed and reported that they had been completely exonerated by the Labor Department, that they ran the most democratic union elections in America. They attacked PACT for daring to challenge a fair election and for wasting the members' money on a baseless challenge. Did they follow the directives of the Labor Department and improve ballot handling procedures? Did they move for greater safeguards on election materials and unused ballots as directed? Of course not. The only change they made in the election rules and processes was *extending* the terms of office from two years to three. This make it even harder for any challengers to keep hope alive. Harder, but not impossible.

Chapter IX.
An Open Letter to CEO Paul Vallas From a Chicago Teacher, 1997

Things became very quiet after the election. Too quiet. The next election was two years away, an eternity. There hadn't been overwhelming interest *during* the campaign. How could we begin to hold the member' interest during the two intervening years, I wondered? A more practical question should have been, how could we begin to hold the committee's interest for two years?

Slowly but surely, our committee members returned to their normal lives and passions and activities and interests. We were spread out all over the city. With no impending crisis, we rarely came together and only talked occasionally. Many times I was alone in writing and putting out a one-page "quarterly newsletter". I hoped that seeing our name a couple of times a year might just keep the PACT idea alive.

A year went by. In May of 1997 I returned again to my initial strategy of having a dinner and seeing who would show up. I invited the committee members and a few new CTU members who impressed me by their words and actions in the House of Delegate' meetings. I had also invited a guest speaker to the dinner. He was someone who was now in a leadership position in another union after his party had been the opposition party for more than ten years. Could he have something to tell us? Could he inspire us to keep at it and give it another try? Could he help us make a difference?

I did find him inspiring, though I definitely did not want to think about being in the opposition for ten years. He shared the story of his caucus. They had begun slowly. They made inroads with their high school teachers. They took over some positions on their union's executive board. They had some kind of action at every union meeting, a motion, an activity, something. They made a name for themselves as getting things done. Ten years later, they were running their union.

Could that happen here, we wondered? It seemed to be such a overwhelming task. Should we try? Fifteen people showed up to that dinner, some who had been in the first campaign, some new. They were all convinced that our union needed new leadership. I was also convinced that we needed more people with us. How to find them?

I had come to believe that a major problem in our 1996 campaign had been the lack of name recognition. Even those who were unhappy with the CTU leadership could be leery of voting for an unknown quantity. We were so small. All of us were full time teachers and school employees with an extremely limited budget and no ability to take off from work to campaign. How could I, we, communicate to a much wider audience who we were and what we stood for?

One idea was for me to lay out a kind of treatise on what I would do if I were president of my union: what I saw as the problems in the system, and how I saw the role of the union and its members in dealing with those problems, and perhaps especially how the union should be positioning its members as the solution to difficulties, not the *cause* of the difficulties. I was frustrated by the CTU leadership's silence and lack of vision and leadership in issues of urban school reform. So I put pen to paper and wrote straight to the CEO of the Chicago Public Schools. I told him what I would have told him had I been the president of my union. If he replied, I could share my letter and his reply with those interested in a change in union leadership. Perhaps PACT would grow that way.

July, 1997
Dear Mr. Vallas,
The students are off for this teacher "professional development" day. We 120 teachers are in the auditorium, sitting on hard, wooden, nailed down seats, for a mandatory six hour workshop on "team-building." Someone in charge, without asking us, decided that we needed this. So the expert told us to turn to our neighbor and tell one thing we had ever done of which we were proud. Then we had to turn to our other neighbor and tell one thing we like about them. Several people were talking while the speaker was lecturing at us. Several people came back late from the morning break. While not very polite, it was perhaps a statement of what they thought about being forced to be there.

Then the team building expert got us. After the break, in a calm, controlled voice, he asked everyone to stand. Then he continued to write four or five rules on the overhead projector: Thou shalt not talk when the speaker is talking. Thou shalt not come back from breaks late, and so on. He asked everyone who could not abide by these rules to sit.

Silence. No one sat. Who would, really, knowing that the principal (who was not present, I might add) would hear about it. With all that established, the speaker then led us, still standing, in a motivational song, and finally asked us to be seated. Despite myself, I felt my hand go up in the air. I was not thrilled with the topic of the day, both for not being involved in the decision and for not seeing how it was going to help us help our majority, at-risk minority kids learn to read (and we did not work in teams anyway). Nevertheless, I had walked into the session with an open mind, trying to make the best of it. Now, despite myself, my hand was raised and my blood was boiling.

"Your little exercise here," I said to the team building expert when he called on me, "felt like punishment, like we were bad children. Perhaps," I continued, "you are punishing the wrong people. Yes, a few people were speaking when they shouldn't have, and yes a few came back late from the break, but we didn't ask to be here. Someone decided that we all needed team building, and whether we want to or not, we

have to be here. Yet we are professionals. This is our professional development day. No one consulted us on how we wanted or needed to be professionally developed. This has nothing to do with you, your subject, or the quality of your presentation, but I think you are blaming the wrong people for what is going on here."

Welcome to the world of Chicago Public School Teachers. The day reminded me of an article I read about twenty years ago, comparing teacher professional development to the insemination of Flossie the cow. The article described teachers being herded into an auditorium, being injected with facts from some outside "expert," (an expert being anyone who lives more than twenty miles away). Like Flossie, they endured, but didn't enjoy it very much. It just happened. Here I was, back in the classroom after a 15-year hiatus working for my union, and it was deja vu all over again.

On that day, 120 teachers spent six hours, at an average rate of pay of $35 per hour. This cost the school $25,300 (not to mention the speaker fee and expenses). The experience did not help us address or advance in our battle with student underachievement. The reason for this is the same reason Chicago school reform, past and present, has failed. No one thought to ask the teachers. Our two recent iterations of Chicago school reform, the 1988 and the 1995 reform bills, both ignored the only thing that matters: *If teaching is going to change, you have to change teaching, and you can't change teaching without the teachers.*

From the outside, teaching looks like a profession and people blame the teachers if their schools are failing. From the inside, however, it isn't a profession at all. We Chicago teachers work in a huge bureaucracy with tens of thousands of employees. It has traditionally been a command and control bureaucracy that needs bureaucrats more than it wants professionals. It wants workers who will do what they are told to do, when they are told to do it and how, they are told to do it. Professionals, on the other hand, lay claim to a body of knowledge. They make decisions based on the needs of the client, not the needs of the bureaucracy.

In their book ***Thinking for a Living***, Ray Marshall and Marc Tucker outline the new survival skills that need to be taught to students: the capacity for abstract thinking skills, the ability to apply this capacity to ambiguous real world problems in a context of constant change, the ability to communicate and work well and easily with others, and to assume responsibility for work without much supervision. If these are the essentials for students, it is easy to see why the old paradigm of command and control of teachers, who have to be the students' role models, won't work.

"Because all students now need to be educated for thinking work, for complex roles as citizens rather than for low skilled factory tasks schools must move beyond their traditional batch and process structures," says nationally renowned researcher Linda Darling Hammond. "If teachers are to succeed...to develop new approaches to curriculum and assessment, work closely and effectively with parent and community organizations, and participate in shaping school policies and practices, they must be prepared to engage in these responsibilities from a deeper base of knowledge and experience." Darling Hammond further states that Advances in our understanding...in many fields make it possible to teach in ways that can enable all students to learn more powerfully and effectively .. If they had access to these understandings, they could become change agents on behalf of their students, themselves and their schools."

These potential change agents should be seen as assets to be listened to and assets to be invested in. If we ever really made an investment in the supply of infinitely skilled teachers we need, and if we ever trusted them with the power and authority to act on that knowledge and expertise in their schools, then it is they and they alone who would turn our schools around.

Yet in Chicago schools, teachers are seen as the problem, not the solution. Yet they are blamed for a reality that they did not make. Teachers simply were not and are not involved in the make-or-break decisions which could turn our schools around. Take the Saturn Model.

Other kinds of organizations, the auto industry, for example, have found out that it's not the people, but the structure and organization and the way that you view employees that can make the difference. One failing American car company in California was taken over by a Japanese company. With the same workers and the same product, but a new style of management that included employee participation and investment in, and respect for, the worker, the Japanese managers were able to turn this company around.

General Motors (GM) and the United Auto Workers (UAW) found the same to be true when the began their Saturn Plant experiment in Spring Hill, Tennessee. Laid off workers from GM went to work at a plant governed, not by the 627-page master GM-UAW agreement, but by a 21-page GM-Local UAW agreement which included such "shared values" as a commitment to customer enthusiasm (not merely satisfaction), a commitment to excel (taking the responsibility but really having the authority via self-managed work teams), teamwork (building on individual talents and encouraging team growth), trust and respect for the worker (dignifying the workers with real authority and trust to do the job), and continuous improvement (recognizing that success hinges on the ability to continually improve the quality of the product and their service).

One example relevant to the discussion of Chicago schools, is their approach to staff development. Everyone in the corporation, including the Saturn president and the local UAW president, is required to spend 5 percent of work time (about 92 hours per year) in training. In fact, 5 percent of their salaries depend on everyone completing the 92 hours. Saturn offers 650 courses developed in total partnership with equal numbers of management and represented workers on the training teams.

How different would Chicago schools be if they operated on these shared values? First, there would be real collaborative decision-making at all levels, from the school system CEO and the union president, all the way down to self managed work teams in the schools. An example of this at the system level for professional development would be that instead of paying untold millions on untried "external partners," university experts and corporate consultants, for what now passes as staff/professional development, there would be a jointly managed (i.e., equal numbers of management and labor) professional development department for the system. This department would, as Saturn has done, jointly develop courses and training programs to be available to the schools. Such programs would be developed by expert practitioners who know the system and know urban schools and therefore would be much more relevant to us than most packaged programs now used. Certain courses could even be approved for carrying undergraduate and graduate credit, allowing paraprofessionals who wanted to be teachers to do so, also. (This would also address looming teacher shortages by increasing the pool of teaching applicants from a group of people who live in and know the communities in which they work. They also have a wealth of skill and knowledge.)

At the school level, the schools would be divided into schools within-schools, small schools under one roof with no more than 300-400 students in each, a concept you are on record as supporting. The idea behind this concept of course, one growing in popularity across the country, is the personalization afforded students and staff. This can be maximized in helping students grow and learn. Yet this structure is as much for the staff as it is for the students. It allows for them to truly work in teams, teams having responsibility for the total education of 300 children, thereby reducing the isolation that characterizes the profession.

Each school would be run by a self-managed work team, say twenty teachers and para-professionals, with its own elected leadership. They would be supported by the principal, assistant principal, counselor and other support staff. The team works by consensus and is responsible for the curriculum and instructional decisions for its students. That is completely different now in that it also has control over the budget, prorated for each school. There would be an overall governing body, again jointly managed with representatives of each small school, which would handle building-wide issues of space and resource allocation. As far as professional development goes, each team, would assess its members' professional development need. The system's academic standards would determine which of the Board's course offerings would best help them achieve the jointly developed goals for improving teaching and learning in their small school that year.

Schools would be judged by how effective the small schools were in meeting the goals, as measured by tests that really assessed them. A major problem with the standardized tests that we currently use is the lack of correlation between what is taught and what is tested. Since presently there are no national standards, there is little commonality between textbooks developed by book publishers for what is taught in various subjects at various grade levels. One district comparison I read about found the overlap between what is in the textbook and what was on the standardized test they used was only 38 percent! Given that Chicago schools are free to select their own textbooks, an anarchy that may not best serve our very transient students, who knows what the overlap is here?

Let's look at teaching, learning and testing in another area for a good example of where teaching to the test is not only not bad, but a good thing. Take swimming lessons, a life or death skill. The American Red Cross has identified certain levels of swimming ability and the various sub-skills required for mastery. Every swimming instructor across the country knows what constitutes the skills for each level. They judge the students on whether they have mastered them before they send them onto the next level. They are tested by showing what they know. The way my children's lessons were organized this summer was instructive: the children were all grouped according to ability (and no parent complained about this kind of tracking). The instructors were assigned to various levels, 1 A, B, C, through 6 A, B, C. The children stayed in their level until their teacher felt that they were ready to be tested. Then another instructor, a tester, would come around and if they agreed that the child had mastered that level, the child passed on to the next level and another teacher.

Everyone involved in the process knew exactly what was expected at every level. The assessment was a performance-the child had to show that they had mastered the skills. The assessment came, not from the teacher but from the tester, which is interesting because it put the teacher and the student into a partnership of learning. They were working together toward a common goal, an attitude usually not found in the classroom because the teacher is the one who grades. Having such standards and assessment did not seem to impinge on the creativity of the swimming instructors, either. Each had their own style and personality and, of course, knowledge and expertise.

Self managed work teams in small schools could use this and other models to create their own versions of schools organized around standards, but the assessments have to be fair. No one would be able to say that teaching to the test is wrong if it were the right kind of test. Teachers would not be afraid of accountability either, if they had what they considered a fair accountability system. That and the power and authority to make decisions in the best interests of teaching and learning. Like the swimming instructors, we classroom teachers too have to teach as if life depended on it, because lives do.

As a teacher in the kind of system I am describing, how would my professional life be different? Let's look again at those "shared values" Saturn's labor and management abide by: commitment to customer enthusiasm, a commitment to excel, teamwork, trust and respect for the worker and continuous improvement. I currently do not feel that I am in a partnership with the Chicago Public Schools (CPS) management to increase my students' love of learning (i.e., customer enthusiasm). I feel that love of learning is getting lost in the stampede for headlines that give the perception to the public that things are changing and that the system is getting rid of bad teachers. CPS management has done nothing but tell me that-first things first- I need a discipline code because I can't be trusted, that "outside experts" know better than teachers how to turn schools around, and that we teachers are responsible for a dysfunctional system we had no say in, that was, in fact, corrupt and mismanaged for decades.

Teachers do not work in teams. We work in isolation behind closed doors. In fact so many of our schools are so big (mine has 2600 students) that faculty members do not even know each other's names. That is why small schools, as good as they are for students, are good for teachers. No teams currently make important decisions. The principal does. I have only as much influence as the principal will allow me to have. It is sad to say that a teacher's entire professional job satisfaction can hinge on whether the person in the principal's office is a benevolent dictator or a despot. As a teacher, the only real decision I make and the only money I have any authority over is the $50.00 annual supply for my classroom.

If I lived and worked under Saturn's values, I would feel valued as a professional. I would feel respected because my voice would be taken seriously and there would be a mechanism for my voice and other voices to be heard and acted upon. I would feel a part of a larger effort that involved me in making the system, the city, a better place. I would feel proud of the responsibility invested in me and would feel that my talents and contributions were recognized and respected. I would be motivated to live up to that responsibility and gladly go the extra mile because I would feel an investment in the school and in the system.

Am I saying that every self-managed team would have all of the answers and turn things around immediately? Not at all. What I am saying is that these people in the trenches know their students, their schools and their communities. They represent the most educated, most experienced teacher work force we have ever had. Do you know how many Chicago teachers have their Master's degrees and doctorates? This is true despite the system's traditional lack of investment in them. They have done it on their own because so many want to continue to grow and learn and better serve our students. What I am saying is that Linda Darling Hammond is right: the knowledge base now exists in substantial part and can be acted upon if (and only if) it is made available to teachers. The only way to make that happen is to invest in the people who can make it happen.

We need a culture of respect for teachers, one we've never had. We need a culture of capacity building and a culture of support for teachers as change agents. Labor can't turn our schools around without management, but management certainly can't do it without labor. Why did GM and UAW restructure their way of doing business in that Saturn plant? Because they had to. Because in the early 80's GM had gone from 65% of the market to about 30%. Their image was so poor that they decided that if they were going to dedicate themselves to getting that market back, they had to start fresh, with a totally new approach. Not one totally untested and unfounded, but one based on research about who was having success. (In their case, it was companies using the Deming model of employee participation and labor management cooperation). With nothing to lose, they agreed to try it.

Just like the auto industry, we need a new way of thinking about unions and their role in turning our schools around. Ironically, while there has been a decline in American unionism, unionism in the countries of our competitors is thriving. In Japan, for example, unions have been integrated into managerial decision making. In Germany, a "codetermination" law mandates union representation on the supervisory boards of all large companies. This suggests, says John Hoerr in his Harvard Business Review article **"What Should Unions Do?"**, *that while a particular kind of unionism may be obsolete, unionism per se, is not.*

"Unions don't have to be obstacles to competitiveness and success," Hoerr states. "Under the right circumstances, they can make a pivotal contribution to them. Much as companies are struggling to define new ways of managing, a new model of unionism is emerging that puts unions at the very center of companies' efforts to improve their competitiveness. In a world where success in the marketplace increasingly depends on creating more flexible, team-based work organizations, unions can be a surprisingly effective means to integrate

employees into managerial decision making. Similarly, the lack of an institution that gives voice to workers' interests and perspectives, can block companies' efforts to adapt to change. Put simply, unions can make stronger companies. To act in this capacity, however, unions must reinvent themselves as much as companies are trying to do."

Harvard law professor Paul C. Weiler sees the decline of unionism as creating a political and legal vacuum, a "governance gap", that damages relationships between workers and managers and the ability to compete. He feels that "union representation is as attractive a form of governance as we have yet been able to devise." He points to two alternatives to unions that have risen to fill the gap, neither of which provides workers with an independent source of power within the organization. One is government regulation, likely to be more of an obstacle to flexibility than unions ever were, and two, the development of human resource programs in organizations. However, these programs are not likely to put workers' interests above the organization's interests.

Why, you might ask at this point, do teachers, if they want to be considered professionals, even need a union? The answer is simple. Management in schools and school systems can be just as arbitrary as management in any other work sector. And teachers, for the very reason that they are or should be professionals, need an independent source of power inside their organizations because the needs of the bureaucracy often conflict with the needs of the profession. Teachers have to have a forum for bringing these conflicts to the surface and to a resolution.

Traditionally, for most teacher unions, these conflicts have been in the realm of bread and butter issues. The union has to react to the initiatives, good or bad, of management. Part of the necessary reinvention of teacher unions has to be expanding the concept of working conditions to include professional issues as well as the traditional ones. Unions need to be pro active rather than reactive in improving the system their members work in. The Toledo Federation of Teachers in

Toledo, Ohio, was one of the first teacher' unions to act on the belief that the union should be as strong on the professional issues as it was on bread and butter issues. The local took the bull by the horns and started with the thorny issue of peer review. It wanted to try to counter the belief that the union only existed to protect bad teachers. It took the local ten years to convince management to establish a jointly run internship program for new teachers and an intervention program for teachers needing remediation. Trained "master" teachers, released from classroom responsibilities for three years, provided support to brand-new teachers and teachers needing help. At the end of a specified period, (one year for interns, one or two for veterans if they were making progress) these master teachers made a recommendation to their Board to retain or release their charges.

And the teachers in Toledo saw this program as one of the best things their union ever did for two reasons: it dispelled the myth that the union was only there to protect bad teachers, and provided unprecedented and meaningful assistance to new and struggling colleagues.

Other teacher unions, such as the United Teachers of Dade (County) in Miami, Florida, The Cincinnati Federation of Teachers and the Rochester, NY Teachers Association have pioneered the concept of shared decision making. While still working to improve this decision-making model, no place has yet to go as far as the Saturn co-management model.

What if we in Chicago committed ourselves to getting our market back, to retrieving the students we have lost and succeeding with the ones we have kept? What if we committed to doing whatever we had to do to achieve it-even co-management? If Saturn workers and management can work together to create a world class car, surely we in the schools should be able to work together to create a world class education for our children. They deserve nothing less. I urge you to consider, on a small scale at first, co-management of just one school, just one region. Let us prove to you that investing trust and

responsibility will reap dividends for the system, for the teachers and for the children who are counting on us.
Sincerely,
Deborah Lynch Walsh
Teacher and CTU Delegate, Marquette Elementary School

I sent my letter in July. August came and went. No answer. Then September. Then October. I realized that I was not going to get a response. That didn't prevent me from sharing my letter. It still represented who I was and what I thought a union should be about. I found a union printer who had a graphic artist on staff. She helped me design and typeset and transform my letter into a sharp, slick-but-classy brochure that I hoped would catch teachers' eyes. Then perhaps my message would capture their attention. At the end of the letter, I added a postscript: "Mr. Vallas never responded to this letter. Perhaps when Ms. Walsh and her caucus are the elected leadership of the Chicago Teachers Union, he will pay more attention to their views."

I then signed a contract to print 10,000 of these brochure-letters. I crossed my fingers and held my breath in the hope that the $4,000 of my own money I was spending would be money well spent. Again I wondered, was anyone out there listening? It didn't take long to find out.

Chapter X.
The PACT Years, 1998-Present: Taking A Stand

I was determined to try again, but not everyone felt as I did.

"Why bother when the UPC controls the election?" many of my PACT friends asked. "Is it really worth going through all that when you have no confidence in the fairness of the process?"

It was difficult to respond. Even if my friends were right, the alternative was even worse. The CTU leadership and its entire UPC caucus would have total control of our union. As it was, thanks to the AFT and the Labor Department, they believed they now had carte blanche to do what they pleased, especially when it came to elections. Still, I just couldn't see giving up and allowing them that victory. The rules *were* unfair, and at least we knew that there were more than 5,000 CTU members who wanted a change. It was a beginning, I argued.

Yet two years was a long time until the next election. (The new three year terms would begin in 1998). We began sending out a quarterly flyer to CTU members on our mailing list, just to keep the PACT name alive. If there was too little interest in the union during an election year, the level of interest in non-election years was barely perceptible. As we went into the 1997 school year—before the May 1998 election—only a third of our original committee members was still involved. Many were still angry about 1996, but many just moved on with other things in their busy, involved lives.

So there we were, just a handful of us starting our monthly meetings in anticipation of the next election. A few developments had occurred since the 1996 election that gave us some hope that another challenge was worth it. In the spring of 1996, Mr. Vallas once again drew on the powers that the Illinois legislature gave him to "reconstitute" underperforming schools. School reconstitution, Chicago style, meant that all staff in seven of our lowest performing (i.e., those with the lowest standardized test scores) were essentially removed from their positions. They had to reapply for them. They did not remove the LSCs. The principals in most cases weren't removed. But in this cynical "reform", moreover, the idea is that it must be the *teachers* who are the problem. This way, management could get rid of the staff members it didn't like, those who raised questions or challenged the status quo.

Overall, 188 teachers from those seven high schools were not rehired. Many of them had received excellent or superior ratings over the years, but that didn't matter. They now became members of a "reserve pool" of teachers who had to substitute four days a week and had Fridays to go around and try to find a position in a school that would have them. This was an absolute travesty for these teachers, many who had taught in schools serving the poorest of the poor for decades. They had dedicated their lives to their students. Yet Mayor Daley and Mr. Vallas had to show the public a "get tough" approach to reforming the toughest-to-reform schools. They did this by getting rid of the "bad teachers."

The press did not reveal, in all its stories about school reconstitution, that these were not the bad teachers. They were just the unwanted teachers who now had to face the humiliation of a scarlet letter on their chest signifying that they came from a reconstituted school. Would principals in the other schools in Chicago be eager (or even willing) to take them? When asked about hiring some of the reconstituted teachers one principal, for example joked that he didn't want someone else's lemons. "I'll hire my own lemons," he commented. That was how many principals felt.

I knew some of these teachers. They were devastated, humiliated, demoralized. With sometimes decades of service, they were now reduced to day-to-day substitute teaching status, begging for a position somewhere. And in the job search, they were essentially on their own. No one was in charge of helping them find another school to work in. The other indignity they faced was the result of another new power of the Board of Education. This was the ability to fire them, even without cause, if they were unable to find a position within ten months. This firing was euphemistically called an "honorable discharge."

And, not surprisingly, there was little or no outcry from our union. We had been warned that reconstitution was coming to Chicago, after prior runs in Baltimore, Philadelphia and San Francisco. And while these other cities were finding out that school reconstitution— replacing senior staff with inexperienced novices and giving them the same poor resources and the same poor management—did not prove to be the panacea they thought, our city was now going to try it. Tom Reece had been quoted in the local newspaper as saying that the CTU wasn't necessarily against reconstitution.

At the March House of Delegates meeting, prior to the June, 1997 reconstitutions, I asked Reece a question about that.

"You have been quoted in the press as saying that the CTU is not against reconstitution. I would like to know on what basis you have taken this position since there has been no discussion on it and no position taken in this House? And also, what are doing to prevent this cynical, anti-union, anti-teacher 'reform' from happening here?"

Predictably, his response was, "That's a political question, and I don't have to answer it." Then he went on to say anyway, "But no one will lose a job in this system." This union leadership had seen this coming and had done nothing, literally nothing to stop it. And, as we well knew, they themselves had no ideas to propose for improving under-performing schools.

At this point I need to describe the CTU House of Delegates meetings. As I mentioned, a large number of the CTU delegates were in the UPC caucus. This caucus usually meets right after the House of Delegates meetings are adjourned. The format of the House meetings includes the reports of the five officers, which usually lasts between one to two hours. Then there is a 15-minute question period for the delegates to get up and speak. Ninety minutes for five people and 15 minutes for 500. And, eager to get on to their UPC meeting, most vote down any motion to extend the 15 minute question period for another 15 minutes. Unbelievable? Yes, but check one out.

Once I became Marquette's delegate (Rudy gracefully bowed out as ours when I told him I was going to run), I used the 15-minute question period to go up and ask tough questions. In the non-election years there were very few people at the microphones. So each month I got up and raised one issue or made a comment on something timely. And each time, just like anyone else who asked a tough question, I would get some kind of dismissive response. Delegates who asked such questions were often hissed by the UPC delegates and ridiculed or yelled at by Reece himself or one of the other officers. Unbelievable? Attend a meeting for yourself.

After a few months of regular opportunities at the microphones during the question period, the UPC members were on to me. They began an effort to race to all the microphones first to try and keep me from getting a chance to speak. Then they would use their time to sing the officer' praises. The best ones at this usually got a full time position at the CTU when vacancies arose. (This was one of the reasons that the current leadership was offended by my working at the CTU. I hadn't come in via UPC channels.) Unbelievable? Ask someone who isn't UPC but who was at these "silence the opposition" sessions.

But my little speeches and this kind of unprofessional and undemocratic treatment were a boon to PACT. Non-UPC delegates (and former UPC delegates) started calling me and joining PACT. They had heard about the shenanigans at the House of Delegate' meetings. They, too, saw that a union that tries to crush dialogue and debate, not to mention opposition, is no union at all.

"That's when I first noticed you," says Sarah Loftus, a current PACT officer. "It was when you got up to ask a logical, rational question about the budget we were about to vote on, and the kind of response you received."

And after reconstitution, the PACT membership list started growing. Our campaign committee started growing, too, leadership spots being filled with energetic and enthusiastic new people, usually school delegates. Soon several PACT delegates were up at the microphones at each meeting, raising issues, asking questions, getting recognized. It became almost comical to see the crush of bodies and the push to the microphones when the question period opened up. Unbelievable? The truth is stranger than fiction.

These House meetings continued to be a forum for PACT members. Otherwise the meetings were deadly dull litanies of officer reports on what meetings they attended and the annual golf outing and bowl-a-thon. There were never any real debates over things like what our position should be on issues like reconstitution, or the employee discipline code, or proactive strategies, like what we advocated for improving the schools we worked in. Many of us would say that if only the members could see what was going on (or not going on) in their union, they'd be appalled. Every chance I had I invited union members to go attend a House of Delegates meeting sometime and see it for themselves. Only a few did.

The PACT campaign committee was moving forward. We could do nothing about the election rules this time, so we concentrated our energies on expanding our base. They couldn't steal the election if the vote was overwhelming, could they? We repeated the theme that it was time for the Chicago Teachers Union to become strong again.

"When Jacqui Vaughn died in 1994, Tom Reece took over the CTU as the caretaker president. No one's heard from him since," began one of our first flyers of the campaign. "On the other hand," the flyer continued, "we've heard from the Board of Education and here is some of what has been said: **Remediation, Reconstitution, Probation, High School Redesign, Employee Discipline Code, Health care Changes in Mid-Contract, Mandated Curricula, Reserve Teacher Policies**...CTU members can't take three more years of 'Silent' Tom Reece."

The issues we stood for included providing articulate and forceful leadership on the issues; fighting for dignity and respect for CTU members; combating reconstitution and winning back our prohibited items of bargaining; and lowering our exorbitant dues while providing better service. Later flyers hit Tom Reece's salary, teacher salaries, and use of dues.

Many members did not realize that Reece was also full-time president of the IFT.

"CTU Members—Are You getting Your Money's Worth? Did You Know That..." began another flyer. "Tom Reece, CTU president, makes more money than his friend, Paul Vallas, than the mayor of the city of Chicago, than the governor of the State of Illinois, and than even the president of the United States, thanks to you." It was true. In 1998 Reece received $102,000 for the CTU job, $75,000 for the IFT position, $24,00 in expense accounts, and the equivalent of 22 percent of his salary in a pension annuity (on top of his Board of Education pension, for union officers are on-leave and still gaining seniority). This didn't include another $25,000 as a mayoral appointee on the Regional Transportation Board. CTU members who saw this flyer were shocked.

Our communication mechanism remained the same as in the previous campaign, i.e., a member in as many schools as possible passing out our materials. By now we had expanded our list from 250 schools to 350 schools. We were also sending our material to the delegates in the additional 230 schools. We hoped that they would do the right thing and share the materials so that their members could decide for themselves. Some did, and some did not. Given our limited finances, it was the best we could do. Besides continuing the school visits before and after school, we mailed 30,000 flyers every month from February through May to get our message out.

We obtained the requisite number of petition signatures for all but two, albeit important, categories. Thankfully, Barbara Hammonds was able to run with us this time. We became the first slate to ever run a paraprofessional for major office in our union. We were very proud of that.

Before we knew it, it was May and time for my ten minutes before the House of Delegates. Many themes and issues remained the same but now had greater urgency when I spoke in May of 1998:

"I come before you today representing thousands of colleagues who understand that we are a union with a proud history that is currently in urgent need of new direction and leadership. Five years ago, Jacqui Vaughn left the CTU a strong, powerful, and influential organization. Politicians and policy makers alike knew that we were a force to be reckoned with. The question is, would Jacqui Vaughn be proud of this union today? If we are honest with ourselves, we know she would not. Since the current leadership has taken over our union has been weakened, our contract gutted, our rights have been eroded, and our dignity impugned. The once powerful CTU has become a virtual afterthought to Paul Vallas and other non-educators as they make critical education decisions which impact every working teacher and paraprofessional.

"Over the past five years, we have been vilified in the press, silenced in the policy making process, and marginalized in our own schools. The current Board leadership is more interested in good public relations for themselves and the mayor than they are in our students and our employees. The current union leadership's tack of collaboration with this Board has been a cruel joke played on every member, and everyone here knows it. Their strategy of appeasement at all costs has

served no one in this union but them, and each of us knows it. While this leadership has enjoyed record-breaking salaries and perks, they have remained astoundingly passive, deafeningly silent—and utterly dishonest. I will address just some of the fictions.

"Fiction #1: In August 1995, Tom Reece said, "The protection of our jobs and our working conditions such as class size have been taken care of in our contract." Fact: We can't bargain class size. Fact: The Board reconstituted seven of our high schools and entire staffs were dismissed and given the 'opportunity' to reapply for their jobs. Fact: Paraprofessionals are now employees at will, with no due process rights in our contract.

"Fiction #2: The current leadership promises that it is going to work with the Board to 'fix' reconstitution. Fact: Reconstitution is an un-fixable, anti-union, anti-teacher travesty, a ploy to replace experienced, senior teachers with less expensive neophyte novices. It is an attempt by the Board to affix the blame of poor standardized test scores on the heads of teachers while ignoring the educational impact of inadequate resources and poor management on our children. The social issues which cause 84 percent of our students (346,000 out of 430,000) to arrive at school underfed, undernourished and under protected are also ignored. Fact: Reconstitution has failed nation wide. When I am elected, reconstitution will have no place in the Chicago Public Schools.

"Fiction #3: The current leadership has told the membership that the health care changes imposed on us in mid-contract would be good for us and not cost additional money. Fact: The health care options now available to the membership have become more limited, while per visit costs have increased...

"Fiction #4: Tom Reece wrote to the membership last month and told us that "The CTU is the most democratic union in the country and has always run fair elections." Fact: When I am elected, it will be. No one in this hall can deny the lack of democracy afforded to you delegates who dare to ask tough questions. This leadership is so afraid of

democracy that, for example, they refused to even allow a discussion of the concept of a mail ballot. When I am elected, this House will become a real deliberative body. Issues will be discussed and all delegates will have legitimate input into the decision making process.

"*Now more than ever we need a union that takes the lead on important issues, instead of bending over for management...PACT commits to the following agenda:*

1. fighting reconstitution and probation, while restoring the dignity and respect our members deserve

2. Providing forceful and articulate leadership...

3. Fighting to win back all of the devastating losses we have suffered...

4. Rebuilding our union: energizing the disillusioned and alienated membership and restoring union democracy...

"*Everyone here knows that if Jacqui Vaughn was still president there would be no reconstitution or probation. CTU members would not be used as political scapegoats, CTU contracts would mean more than the paper they were written on. Tom Reece has been unable to effectively carry on the CTU tradition of dignity and respect for all members. It's time for a change. The PACT slate will make the CTU a union we can all be proud of again. It's time to take back our union. Thank you.*"

I could feel it as I stepped away from the podium. The rising applause. The sustained, strong reaction to what I had said. This despite the large number of UPC members in the room. I could tell that it was much stronger than it had been two years ago. Was this a sign? Did we have a chance?

This time the UPC couldn't portray PACT as a one woman show. This time they attacked "the phone calls, missives and disruptive behavior in the House of Delegates" and stated that "We (the UPC) are not reactive. We're not even pro active. We're the active leadership caucus of the CTU." and "The opposition lacks experience, led by a candidate who lost overwhelmingly when she ran against us two years ago." "We wonder if she ever filed a grievance for anyone in her school" stated another piece.

The incumbents *did* use the Labor Departments report to their advantage. In a letter to the entire membership, at union expense, Reece stated that we alleged that the delegates did not conduct honest elections, a charge totally untrue. It was meant to inflame the delegates against us. He failed to identify where the Department had alleged violation of the CTU Constitution and federal election law. He only quoted the Department's decision that legal action was not warranted and they were closing the file. "Ms. Walsh failed to accept the decision of the AFT and submitted her complaints to the United States Secretary of Labor...Unfortunately, thousands of dollars of dues money and hundreds of hours of staff time were expended in what we knew were legal elections. The May 1998 CTU election will be conducted fairly and honestly, as always...Thank you for helping to make the Chicago Teachers Union the most democratic union in the country."

Mr. Despres *again* came to our aid. He sent Reece a letter stating that his letter unfairly impugned our challenge, misstated the results of the Department of Labor investigation and implied that there was something improper or disloyal about a member seeking to ensure that elections are fairly conducted. He concluded that Reece's letter, "printed on union stationery and apparently paid for with union funds, may constitute campaign literature and, as such, may be a violation of CTU rules, if not the Labor Management Reporting and Disclosure Act itself."

Reece never responded.

I wasn't too concerned about the impact of that letter. Once again Reece himself had publicized my name to the entire membership. How much could the accusation that I was pressing for a fair election hurt us? It was what he and his cohorts did one week before the election that made me realize that our efforts this second time before CTU voters were doomed.

That Friday before the May 20, 1998 election we received the monthly *Chicago Union Teacher*, the CTU newspaper that goes to each member. Tradition also dictated that the biographies of all the candidates for local office were printed in the May issue in an election year. As delegate, the newspaper came to me and I began placing them in the staff mailboxes. At one point, curious, I opened a copy to see how the bios looked. When I got to mine, I almost fainted.

There instead of the biography I had submitted, was a greatly shortened version of who I was supposed to be. It started with the words "CTU member since 1991." They had slashed and trashed my biography and the biographies of several PACT candidates. In my case they had rewritten history, fabricated dates and deleted information that they feared might encourage someone to vote for me.

Once again, the law offices of Despres and Geoghegan came to our support. That afternoon Sarah Vanderwicken, a lawyer in the firm, shot off the following letter:

"Dear Mr. Reece,

"The May issue of the Chicago Union Teacher, *which is published under your supervision and control, purports to set out the biographical statements submitted by candidates in the CTU election. It states that 'biographies are printed as submitted without editing except for personal information'."*

"The claim not to have edited the submissions is absolutely false. Not only has significant information been deleted, but information provided in the submissions has actually been changed in the printed version, obviously to suit the interests of the incumbent slate. As one example, the submission by Deborah Walsh was cut over a third, from 967 words to 632. Among other things, the printed copy deleted the highly relevant information that Ms. Walsh was a member of the CTU from 1974 through 1979, stating instead that she had only been a member since 1991, excised information showing her association with former CTU president Jacqueline Vaughn, and essentially rewrote her statement, changing the tone as well as the information contained

therein. *These and other changes to candidate statements are obviously an effort to support your attempts to falsely paint the PACT candidates as inexperienced neophytes and to prevent the members from learning the truth.*

"In the same issue CTU members are falsely informed that the Labor Department completely exonerated you in its investigation of the conduct of the previous election, rather than that the department determined that the various improprieties it found failed to warrant a reelection because they did not appear to be capable of affecting the results of the election.

"No such defense could be asserted about the gross alteration of the biographies submitted by PACT candidates. There is no way you will be able to prove that this alteration did not contaminate the election, since this issue of the Chicago Union Teacher *is reaching members right before the election and provides the most information most members receive about the candidates.*

"The outrageous wholesale reediting of the biographies submitted by PACT candidates requires either that 1.) The UPC slate or whoever else was responsible for this conduct send out a corrected copy to CTU members, at its expense, or 2.) The election itself be postponed. Anything less makes a mockery of a claim that this is a fair election."

Reece never responded to that letter either.

I knew that this trick was the death knell for our challenge. Chicago is a town where you have to pay your dues to prove yourself. Any member who didn't know me (and with 33,000 members, which was quite a few) was not about to vote for an unknown person who had only been in the system since 1991. Not only that, they had deleted information about my extensive work with paraprofessionals while at the AFT, my teaching experience at the University of Illinois-Chicago, my membership and activism in the AFT staff union, and more. Anything that might make me look like a viable candidate. And mine wasn't the only one. Our last flyer had just gone out when the union papers arrived in the schools, carefully timed to arrive the week of the election. We were out of money and out of time, helpless to counter this injustice.

Election day finally came. Same process, same concerns. Only this time they had shown such a total disregard for election fairness with the bio tampering, the election process itself was secondary. When the totals came in four days later our reaction was bittersweet. We had lost the city-wide offices, but PACT had made tremendous advances. Whereas we won 28 percent of the vote the first time around, this time we won 42.5 percent! We had made substantial inroads into the UPC's support. Even better, *all* PACT candidates for high school seats on the CTU executive board had won! We had carried the high schools by 70 percent of the vote! No caucus had ever broken into power like this in 30 years. We were inside the door, the inner sanctum of CTU politics. It was the beginning of our official union leadership. I knew right there that we couldn't stop now. All we needed was 51 percent. If we just continued to grow as we had been growing, and the UPC continued to lead as it had been leading, then the next time we would have it. We were in, not totally, but in nevertheless.

"**Reece is reelected, but opposition gains**" read the headline in the *Chicago Tribune*. "Reece's victory is down from two years ago against the same challenger...Walsh and her slate had said that Reece was too cooperative with school board officials as they reconstituted high schools and a few elementary schools, which included transferring teachers from those schools. Reece attributed the six losses to 'residual bitternes' about those reconstitutions."

I went back to Marquette with my head held high. We had our own campaign there to increase student achievement. That would certainly keep me challenged and well-occupied for the next three years, until the next election.

More people than ever before began coming to PACT meetings *after* we had lost. They, too, could feel it. They, too, had a feeling that next time might be the right time. We had lost, but now we were excited and proud of ourselves. PACT was stronger than ever. We could do it. Yes we would challenge the unfairness of this election, the use of union funds to campaign, the biography bashing. Nevertheless, we knew that would take time. We would continue to work for election fairness. PACT now had six voices on the union's executive board. We would continue to reach out and expand our base. PACT had strong support in the high schools, and we had to work to keep it. We had to figure out a more effective way to reach the elementary school members and the paraprofessionals.

Shortly after this election, Mr. Vallas moved again to exercise even more of the powers that the 1995 legislation enacted. First, he postponed the ten-month limit on the reserve teachers from those reconstituted schools until past Reece's election. He postponed it again to ensure a contract settlement. Nevertheless, he fired 138 CTU members *without cause* and when there *were* vacancies in their fields. This was unprecedented in CTU history. Again, the Reece team was helpless to prevent this or to do anything about it. Reece's promise that "no member would lose his or her position in this system," ended up being empty campaign rhetoric. "Seniority is dead in this system," cried Paul Vallas at a Board of Education meeting where PACT leaders were protesting the firings. "The only way it will ever come back is by changing the law."

To change the law, you have to have leadership. You have to have public support. The public will only be on your side if they believe that you are working in the interests of the children. One of our slogans during the second campaign was "Good working conditions are good learning conditions." The union leadership needs to communicate that, and communicate the stories of all the heroes in our public schools. No, not all school staff members are heroes, and the union should have a position on (and a program for) that, too. You have to build relationships with the politicians and policy makers and find common ground on your issues. You have to *have* issues and ideas and a vision of how to improve things. You have to stand for something. Are we workers or are we professionals? Is improving the schools management's job or our job? Is true collaboration with management union leadership, or union sellout? These and other questions need to be grappled with. The jury is still out about what Chicago teachers, and teachers across the country, will ultimately choose. I want to be part of that decision.

Epilogue

It is now the year 2000. As I look back at my 25-year career in education, I am happy with the decision I made a quarter of a century ago to enter the teaching profession. It is challenging, usually satisfying, sometimes frustrating, but never boring work in the service of children and their families.

My own little family has grown. Barb's children—my children, are now nine, eleven and thirteen years old. They are happy, typical, fun-loving kids, a testament to the love and support of our tight and loyal extended family. We still live in the suburbs to be near that family and my now-widowed mother, with whom I am very close. She has been an incredible support and has shown an unbelievable strength of spirit and resolve in the face of many cruel losses.

I recently married Bill Byrne, a co-worker from Marquette School, the building's operating engineer and an officer in his *own* union. Bill was a widower when we met, with a teen-aged daughter. Together we are raising our four great children. My mother used to jokingly say that only a saint would marry a woman with three small children. I was lucky enough to find a man with a heart big enough for all of us. The fact that he made a generous donation to the first PACT campaign early in our relationship didn't hurt either. He still says that it was the best investment he ever made.

Being a parent has enhanced my teaching tremendously. I can see—from a parent's perspective—how much a kind word from a teacher (or a careless criticism), can mean to a child. I know how much it takes to send them off each day, ready and eager and prepared. I know what I expect from their teachers and their schools, and this standard has guided me in my work. I simply can't give my students anything less than what I want for my own. I think that's what a sense of community is all about. Though I am a strong advocate for public schools, my own children attend a Catholic school. I had had many academic "public versus private school" discussions with my sister. She ultimately chose a Catholic school and the fact that they still attend a Catholic school is my effort to honor her wishes.

At Marquette, we are hard at work at trying to make a success of Success for All. Since we have embarked on that challenge, I find it much more rewarding to work there. I now feel a real sense of collegiality as we all take a chance, together, on something new. There is a deeper sense of satisfaction in the work. Teaching is not so isolated anymore. We meet and talk all the time now. We have a common mission. I know my colleagues so much better now. We have a *reason* to talk professionally, and we get to know each other better personally, as well. There is a real sense of *professional* community. Since our students change reading groups as often as every eight weeks, we share many of the same children. You start caring about more than simply those students in your own class. There is a real sense of *school* community, as well.

As for the teaching profession, however, I wonder if the glass is half empty or half full. For example, everything we have done at Marquette still remains at the mercy of the person in the principal's office. Things still sometimes happen at the school against the wishes of the staff. If the principal wants to keep a program, the principal can keep it. If not, as we saw happen at the first Chicago SFA school we first visited, the whim of a new principal coming in with her own ideas ends up meaning more than the wishes of the faculty.

One of the classes I now teach at the university is an undergraduate course called "The School in Society." As I work with these bright students—eager, excited, and even a little scared to be teachers—I ask myself if encouraging them to become teachers is the right thing. Teacher power and powerlessness are as much issues today as they were 25 years ago when I started. But maybe now the time is riper for teacher empowerment. As reform after reform with disempowered teachers fails, perhaps the realization that, that only reform with empowered teachers is strong and lasting will prevail.

I tell my undergraduate students that they must be advocates for their students **and** their profession as they venture forth to save the world. I encourage them to become activists for themselves and their students in their classrooms, in their schools, and in their union. This makes me feel better about encouraging them to enter the profession.

For I sincerely believe that the union is the only hope for teachers. If teachers want true empowerment, then we have to fight for it. I know for sure that it will never be handed to us. We teacher union members have to believe that we are worth trust and leadership and equality, from our employer *and* from our union. The CTU has to have union leadership that believes this also. That is why Chicago teachers and educational paraprofessionals are at a crossroads. They face a crucial decision. Will they empower themselves and their union to seek professional status at the bargaining table and in the schools? Will they seek to claim their rightful place among the more lucrative (and more male dominated) professions? Will they courageously fight for what is right?

Just as well known writers face hundreds, sometimes thousands, of rejections before they get their work published, as pioneering researchers face endless dead ends and failures before they make scientific breakthroughs, and well-loved baseball players weather defeat after defeat but persevere and take the championship, so too will the members of PACT relentlessly carry on in the name of teacher dignity and respect. For the numbers are on our side.

When we were the little known voice of change in our first challenge, we still marshaled nearly 30 percent of Chicago teachers' and (paraprofessionals') votes. When the stakes became even higher for staff in the school system, and that voice became louder and our names a little more recognizable, we won 42 percent of the votes of CTU members. We also won all six of the high school positions on the 40-member CTU Executive Board, becoming the voice for *all* of the high school teachers. Next time will be the charm. Next time we will take over the leadership of the Chicago Teachers Union and lay claim to that dignity and respect CTU members deserve.

For if we teachers do not believe in ourselves, who will believe in us? If we union members and union activists do not believe in ourselves, who will? It's just like the well-loved labor union song, *Solidarity Forever*, says. "What force on earth is feebler than the feeble strength of one? For the union makes us strong."

About the Author

Deborah Lynch Walsh is a Chicago Public School teacher, an activist in the Chicago Teachers Union, and an advocate for teacher empowerment and education reform. She holds a B.S. degree in Elementary and Special Education from Western Illinois University, an M.S. degree in Special Education from Chicago State University, and a Ph.D. in Educational Policy Analysis from the University of Illinois-Chicago. She has taught 11 years at the elementary level, 11 years at the college level, and has worked for both the American Federation of Teachers, and the Chicago Teachers Union. She lives with her husband and four children in metropolitan Chicago.

9 780595 097203